Phenomenal Family

Phenomenal Family
Treats, Traditions, and Activities

By

MITZI DEETER

CFI
Springville, Utah

ISBN 13: 978-1-59955-198-2

Published by CFI, an imprint of Cedar Fort, Inc., 2373 W. 700 S., Springville, UT 84663
Distributed by Cedar Fort, Inc., www.cedarfort.com

LIBRARY OF CONGRESS CATALOGING-IN-PUBLICATION DATA

Deeter, Mitzi, 1969-
  Phenomenal family : treats, traditions, and activities / Mitzi Deeter.
    p. cm.
  ISBN 978-1-59955-198-2
  1. Family–Miscellanea. 2. Manners and customs. 3. Rites and ceremonies.
  4. Family festivals. I. Title.
  HQ734.D429 2008
  394.2--dc22
                              2008027805

Cover design by Nicole Williams
Cover design © 2008 by Lyle Mortimer
Edited and typeset by Natalie A. Hepworth

Printed in the United States of America

10 9 8 7 6 5 4 3 2 1

Printed on acid-free paper

Dedicated to my family.

Table of Contents

Acknowledgments

I would like to thank my husband, Brian, and my children, Allyson, Karlee, Lynzi, and Dustin for their patience and love. They put up with all of my crazy ideas and they make family life great! I would also like to thank my mom for the many hours she spent helping me.

Family First

Making Your Family a Priority

amily. This one word brings feelings of comfort, unconditional love, and acceptance. We are all part of a family and if asked, many of us would say that our family is the most important aspect of our lives. In this crazy world our families are pulled in many directions. We hardly have time to be with the ones we love most.

If family truly is the most important aspect in your life, then take the steps to make them a priority. Put first things first!

This chapter has suggestions on how to put family first.

COMMIT TO FAMILY NIGHT

Schedule one night each week to devote to your family. Family night should be a time when you give undivided attention to your family. You can teach a lesson and have an activity and a treat.

If you are fully committed to this family time, it will be a night when all of your children are at home. On this night they will not attend other activities or go to friends' homes. As a parent, don't plan work or social meetings on this night. Oprah Winfrey once said, "If you don't have the time for one night or at least one hour during the week where everybody can come together as a family, then the family is not the priority." (Covey, Stephen R., *The 7 Habits of Highly Effective Families* [New York: Macmillan, 1997], 113). Do what it takes, and get started now!

You will find ideas for lessons, games, and activities in the following chapters. Also, take a look at the mealtime and tradition chapters to enhance your family night.

CHOOSE TO PUT FAMILY FIRST

Get schedules of your children's extracurricular events. Attend these events together as a family. It doesn't matter if your children have a small part in the event. What matters is that you are there to support them.

Schedule time to be with your family as if you were scheduling an important business meeting. Keep your family appointments.

ONE-ON-ONE TIME

Spend one-on-one time with each child and with your spouse. One-on-one time allows you to connect with each member of your family individually and give everyone the message that they are important to you.

Look in the chapters Marriage Matters and Connecting With Kids for ideas for one-on-one time.

PLAN

Make goals as a family. Write down these goals and refer to them often. Write a family mission statement that speaks of the ultimate plan for your family. In the chapter on compiling a family book, you can get several ideas on how to set, plan, and accomplish goals.

To those who would say, "We don't have time to do these things!" I would say, "You don't have time not to!" The key is to *plan ahead and be strong* (Covey, Stephen R., *The 7 Habits of Highly Effective Families* [New York: Macmillan, 1997], 162-163).

GET AWAY FROM IT ALL

Family vacations are great memory makers. Make sure you plan at least one family vacation each year. Plan in advance so you can build anticipation. Families who go camping together truly grow together. Think about it: no television, no telephone, and no running back and forth to friends' houses. Imagine spending a full week or even a few days with family, enjoying nature, working together, and having a good time. What could be better?

Week-long getaways bring excitement to the family, too. Whether you like to go to the beach, city, mountains, or out of the country, spending a week without the pressures of work, school, or other commitments is wonderful!

CREATE

A phenomenal family does not create itself. You must "decide to actively . . . work on improving your family situation each and every day . . . [and then] 'do it,' every single day" (McGraw, Dr. Phil, *Family First: Your Step-by-step Plan for Creating a Phenomenal Family* [New York: Simon and Schuster, 2004], 33).

A tried-and-true formula fits the bill here: be, do, have. *Be* committed, *do* what it takes, and you will *have* what you want.

If your schedule does not permit you to spend quality time with your family, change your schedule. Family is that important! Create opportunities and moments with your family.

BROADEN YOUR HORIZONS

Present many different experiences for your family, such as music, art, drama, literature, science, leadership, travel, sports, service, cooking, cleaning, and automobile maintenance. Exposing your family to many activities might help them discover new talents and interests. Do not over-schedule your children with too many activities. Create a family environment that allows them time to relax and enjoy being home.

MAKE HOME A PLACE THEY WANT TO BE

Home should be a place where peace, safety, and love abound. Home should also be a place where there is a predictable schedule. It is where values are taught and lived. In the chapter Making Home a Haven, many ideas are given on how to make your home a safe haven for your family.

Invite friends over, plan activities, and provide food for them. Make your home a place where your family and friends would like to be.

COMMUNICATE

Talk about things with your family. Show your family that you will honestly listen to them. Answer any questions they might have or try to find answers to their questions. Even talk about trivial things. Ask questions to find out about each individual in your family. Work together and talk while you work. Really get to know your family.

Catch your children doing something good and let them know that you notice!

STRENGTHEN FAMILY

Regularly strengthen and build the storehouse of self-esteem in each family member. Commend more than you correct.

Strengthen each family member with love, gratitude, and kindness.

Include your extended family. There are many ideas in the chapter Extended Family Network.

Teach values and doctrine daily and live after the manner of happiness. Dedicate your home as a place that is not of the world.

PERSONALIZE

You know your family and your family's needs better than anyone. The steps in this book are given to get your ideas flowing. I encourage you to choose, commit, plan, communicate, strengthen, and create a family that is first in your life.

Enjoy each moment with the ones you love most. . . *family.*

Marriage Matters

If You Love Em, Tell Em

The greatest gift we can give our children is a loving relationship with our spouse.

A happy and respectful marriage relationship brings peace and security to children. Happiness in marriage is not something that just happens. A good marriage must be created. In the art of marriage, the little things are the big things. Marriage is the following:

- Never being too old to hold hands
- Remembering to say "I love you"
- Forming a circle of love that includes the whole family
- Demonstrating gratitude in thoughtful ways
- Having the capacity to forgive and forget
- Giving each other an atmosphere in which each can grow
- Not only marrying the right partner, but being the right partner

The divorce rate in America is over 60 percent. It is very important to make your spouse high on your priority list.

This section of the book provides ideas to make your spouse feel spoiled and loved.

RECIPE FOR A HAPPY MARRIAGE
  1 cup love and friendship
  2 cups loyalty
  3 cups forgiveness
  5 spoons hope and tenderness
  4 quarts faith
  1 barrel laughter

5

Take love and loyalty and mix them thoroughly with faith. Blend with tenderness, kindness, and understanding. Add friendship and hope. Sprinkle abundantly with laughter. Bake it with sunshine, and serve generously daily.

SIXTY-SECOND MIRACLE

A psychotherapist began prescribing sixty-second hugs for nearly half of his patients and saw amazing results. Calling it the sixty-second miracle, he found that the hug reduces stress, helps induce fun, opens up communication, and encourages forgiveness between husbands and wives. Here's how to do it:

1. Let yourself go; don't be embarrassed
2. Have no preconceived expectations (this is harder for men)
3. Seek permission before you hug your partner
4. Agree on the length of time involved
5. Begin with trust

See if you too can have a sixty-second miracle.

FIVE IMPORTANT QUESTIONS

1. Am I able to think of the interest of my marriage and partner first before I think of my own desires?
2. How deep is my commitment to my companion, aside from any other interests?
3. Is my spouse my best friend?
4. Do I have respect for my partner as a person with worth and value?
5. Is there a spiritual bond between us?

The answers to these questions should pull couples together, not apart.

DATE BOOK

Here are some great ideas to make sure you and your spouse are spending enough time together. Fill a book with dates you can go on throughout the year and use the ideas when planning a night out. Following are some ideas for dates:

- Buy season tickets for a play or a sports team. Put all the dates of the plays or games in your date book.
- Purchase movie and dinner gift certificates.
- Go for a walk to a park and feed the birds.
- Play computer games.

- Try out a new restaurant.
- Attend a high school ball game, concert, or play.
- Go to the library or a bookstore and just browse.
- Invite friends over and play games.
- Go on a picnic and a hike.
- Take a class together such as dance, computer, gardening, or religion.
- Go bowling, or play miniature golf or ping-pong.
- Revert to being a kid by flying a kite, putting puzzles together, building a sand castle, going to the zoo, or swinging at the park.
- Design your dream home or go test-drive new cars. It never hurts to dream!
- Find a museum or visitors' center and take a tour.
- Rent a video and have video night with popcorn and treats.
- Take a moonlight walk, ski, or swim.
- Make dinner together and eat it by candlelight.
- Rent a tandem bike, motor scooter, or four-wheeler and go for a ride.
- Go on your first date again by eating the same thing and going where you went.
- Invite your spouse home for lunch on a work day.

POCKET SURPRISES

Fill your spouse's pockets with surprises. Fill the pockets that he will see that day or fill pockets that they will find at unexpected times. Here are some ideas for your spouse's pockets:

- Put a love note in a shirt or pants pocket.
- Stuff a coupon for a special treat in a purse or wallet.
- Put a candy treat in a seat pocket or visor in his car.
- Leave a note in a day timer or journal.
- Stuff a note or surprise in his briefcase, bag, or wallet.
- Text him a message or send an email.

PILLOW PRESENTS

Take turns leaving something you know your spouse would like on each other's pillows. The rule is that you alternate pillow presents, so once you get it you need to pass it on.

- Cut out colored hearts and write little "I love you" notes on each of the hearts. Put the notes all over your spouse's pillow. On one heart let them know that they just had a "heart attack."

- Put a CD of favorite songs on his pillow.
- Place a coupon for a back rub or a bubble bath on your spouse's pillow.
- Wrap a bottle of perfume or cologne and place it on his pillow.

SCAVENGER AND TREASURE HUNTS

- Draw a map and have it delivered to him with instructions to follow the map to the treasure. This map should take him to you. Find a place out of the way such as the mountains, a field, or a park. When he arrives have his favorite dinner, lit candles, and lots of blankets. Take along anything you need to make your evening cozy.
- Go to a grocery store and get all of the clerks to help you. Your spouse will be instructed to go to a certain clerk. That clerk will give him an item that he will need and the name of the next clerk. When he gets home, he should have everything needed to make dinner.
- Hand your spouse an item and ask him to put it away. When he puts that item away there will be something else out of place with a note telling him to put that item away. Continue until the last item, which is a treasure.
- Call with instructions to go to a restaurant and pick up an item. At that restaurant there will be a note with instructions to go to another place and pick up an item for your evening together. The last clue will lead your spouse to you. Spend the evening together with the collected items.
- A "whoops, no restaurant" April Fool's Day hunt. Tell your spouse to meet you for an elegant dinner. Give an address but no name of the location. When he gets there, he'll find nothing but an old parking lot or empty building. Set up a card table with your finest linen, crystal and china. Dress to kill, and enjoy a candlelit dinner in the middle of nowhere.
- Make a puzzle that your spouse will have to put together. This puzzle will lead him to where you have a treasure.
- Clues for treasure hunts could be left in a mailbox, on the computer screen, or on the answering machine. Or a phone

number could be given that your spouse can call. Have a person on the other end that gives him the clues.

- Plan a treasure hunt through your house. Leave the first clue on the door as he enters. Hide with your kids in the closet with his favorite treat in your hand. Send him around your house before he finds you.

FUN AT THE OFFICE

It is always nice to get a surprise at work to remind you that you are loved. Here are some things you can do at your spouse's workplace to make his day brighter:

- Mail a package to his work or take it to a secretary to place on his desk. Make sure it looks like a mailed package; you want to catch your spouse off guard. Don't let the package appear to be a gift. Whatever you put in the package should remind him for the rest of the day that he has you and he can't wait to get home.
- Decorate his office for holidays, a special occasion, or for no reason at all. Put hearts on the door and fill a candy dish with his favorites. Have a photograph of you and the kids taken and leave it on his desk.
- Make a calendar that has pictures of the family for him to see all year long.
- Mail a card or letter to his work.
- Go to his office and bring him lunch.
- Have flowers delivered.
- Hide a surprise in a desk drawer that he will find later.
- Call him and let him know you are thinking of him. Don't ask him to do anything like pick up groceries. This is strictly an "I love you" call.
- Have a professional take your picture and give it to your spouse for the office.
- Write little messages on post-it notes and place them all over the office.
- Have someone set a box of chocolates on his desk. The surprise comes when he goes to eat the chocolates and finds an unexpected surprise inside instead of chocolates. You could write a note that says your chocolates are waiting at home for you. Rewrap the chocolates before you give them to him.

AT HOME ROMANCE

Remember, little gestures go a long way in the romance department. A simple note, treat, or gesture can make your spouse's day. Following are a few ideas of small gestures to bring a smile to his face:

- Sprinkle the floor from your bed to the shower with chocolate candy kisses. When your spouse gets out of bed, he will see the kisses. When he gets into the shower have a note there saying, "I kiss the ground you walk on and shower you with love."
- Buy ten poster boards that are the same color. With a marker write messages on the posters like, "Hey good looking," "What a babe," and "You take my breath away." Post the posters on telephone poles that you know your spouse will be driving by that day. If you are traveling with your spouse make sure to point out the signs and make a big deal of them, but don't let him know the signs are for him. That night before you go to bed, pull out a poster that confirms he's that good looking babe that takes your breath away.
- Physically connect with your spouse, look at him, hold his hand, kiss him, hug him, and sit by him. Make sure he knows there is no one else you would rather be with.
- Tell your spouse you love him in different ways: pull the silverware out of the drawer and spell I love you with forks, knives, and spoons. Kiss the bathroom mirror and write a lipstick note.
- Tape notes around the house. For example, hang a note that says "I light up when you are near," on the light switch, "You have the key to my heart," on the key holder, and "You are music to my ears," on the stereo or piano.
- Get a babysitter who will watch your kids and plan a romantic evening at home. You could do a different activity in each room, such as dinner in the kitchen, a movie in the family room, games in the closet, and a hot bath in the bathroom.

SHOCK YOUR SPOUSE

Do something your spouse has been begging you to do.

- Finish a household project.
- Be spontaneous. Jump into the car and go where the wind blows.
- Deliver a key to a hotel room and a note for him to meet you there for lunch.

- Put on bright red lipstick and give him a kiss when he is asleep. He'll get a surprise when he looks in the mirror.

CANDY CARE PACKAGES

Candy is an easy and inexpensive way to deliver a fun surprise to your spouse. Some ideas for candy care packages are:

- Personalize candy by making a wrapper for a candy bar that has a love message from you. You can even personalize M&M's with your own message on it. Go to www.mymms.com to order.
- Make a card with candy conversation hearts. You can come up with a message unique to your relationship.
- Make a candy bar poster or write notes with candy bars.
  › *Gum.* I chews you
  › *Snickers.* You make me snicker
  › *Big Hunk.* To my big hunk
  › *Mamba.* You're one hot mamba
  › *Twix.* I'm in a twix without you
  › *Tootsie Roll.* Hey, tootsie, I love you
  › *U-no.* U-no how great I think you are
  › *Reeses Pieces.* I love you to pieces
  › *Skor.* You skor high with me
  › *Swedish Fish.* Of all the fish in the sea, you're the one for me
  › *Nestlé Treasure.* I treasure you
  › *M&M's.* You're my macho man
  › *Sugar Babies.* Be my sugar baby
  › *Hugs & Kisses.* XOXOXO
  › *Starburst.* You make me see stars

FOOD FUN

- Make a cookie bouquet. Purchase flower-shaped cookies with holes in the middle and get large gumdrops and bamboo skewers. To make flowers, skewer a gumdrop, then put the cookie on, and then add another gumdrop. Place the cookie flowers in a flower pot. Add ribbon, baby's breath, or fern for a festive look.
- Bake your spouse's favorite treat.
- Use canned food, fruit, or other foods to share a fun message.
  › *Mandarin oranges.* Orange you glad we're together.

> › *Can of nuts.* I'm nuts about you.
> › *Artichoke hearts.* You're always in my heart.
> › *Olives.* I love you. (olive you)
> › *Soup.* You're Super.
> › *Honey dew.* Honey do you know how much I love you?
> › *Apple.* You're the apple of my eye.
> › *Melon.* I love you for a million (melon) different reasons.
> › *Pizza.* You have a piece of my heart.

NOTES, NOTES, NOTES

- Write a note in his journal. The next time he writes in his journal he will get a surprise from you.
- Think ahead and send your Valentine letter to Loveland Colorado. It will be hand-stamped with a unique four-lined poem. The Loveland Chamber of Commerce heads up this yearly romance project with cards going to all fifty states and over one hundred countries annually. It's simple. Just enclose your pre-addressed, pre-stamped card in a larger envelope and mail to:

  Postmaster
  Attn: Valentines
  Loveland, CO 80537

Note: You can also send your letter to postmasters of these cities:

> › Valentine, Texas 79854
> › Valentine, Nebraska 69201
> › Kissimmee, Florida 32741
> › Loving, New Mexico 88256
> › Bridal Veil, Oregon 97010
> › Romance, Arkansas 72136

- Create love coupons for breakfast in bed, a bubble bath, car wash, back rub, to pick the next movie, sleep in day, ultimate nap (do not disturb), weekend getaway, and full day of total control over the remote.
- Write a note in the snow by coloring water and spraying it in the snow.
- Plant your garden in the shape of a heart.
- Email a card. There are many great websites that have premade email cards and videos. A few websites are: www.americangreetings.com, and www.hallmark.com.

- Count out how many days you have been married and send a card saying, "Happy 2,349 Anniversary Day!"
- Fill a jar full of 365 notes: one for every day of the year. The notes should all start out with "I love you for . . ." and think of 365 reasons why you love him.

VIP CERTIFICATE

Make a certificate that says, "Very Important Person Award presented to: (spouse's name). Be it hereby recognized that the above named person is the Very Important Person in my life, by virtue of many demonstrated acts, among which are these:

1. Always being there when I need you.
2. Understanding my moods and knowing my deepest desires.
3. Loving me when I am up, down, or in between.
4. Being a source of patience, love, and strength, even when I am irrational.
5. Somehow always bringing out the best in me.
6. Even when taken for granted by me, continuing to provide for the needs and desires of the unpredictable creature I am.

In grateful acknowledgement by all of the above, this award is given this _____ day of _____

Signed (your name)

KIDNAP YOUR SPOUSE

- Arrange your spouse's schedule, pack for him, and then go and take him from work. Head out of town for a weekend away.
- Blindfold your spouse and drive him around to get him confused. Lead him to a spot where you have prepared dinner and an evening of fun.
- Send an invitation to your spouse asking him on a date. Make the invitation mysterious as to where you are going or what you are going to do. When the day of the date comes, send little notes and reminders of the great date you have planned; the anticipation is the best part. When you go on the date, blindfold him and take him around the neighborhood to confuse him. Come back home and in your backyard have a tent set up with dinner and a movie. He still doesn't know where you are. After the movie, disclose the location of your date.

THE DAILY DOZEN

This daily dozen will enhance your romance if used faithfully on a daily basis.

1. Spend five minutes every day thinking positive thoughts about your spouse.
2. Pay your partner a genuine compliment.
3. Give your partner a gesture of love.
4. Be supportive.
5. Spend ten to fifteen minutes each day communicating your feelings with your spouse.
6. Listen and give respect to your partner's ideas and suggestions.
7. Laugh at yourself because you can't worry and laugh at the same time.
8. Be positive.
9. Make home a sanctuary.
10. Make time for each of you to be alone.
11. Give your spouse a break.
12. Give of yourself and then give some more.

BOOKS

Books are a great way to express how you feel. They also make wonderful keepsakes. The following are some book ideas to give to your spouse:

- *Birthday Scrapbook.* Think of qualities that you love about your spouse. Find pictures of him that go with these qualities. Use pictures from his childhood as well as present-day pictures. Find a quote or poem that goes with the quality. Make scrapbook pages with the quote, the picture, and the quality. Do as many qualities as your spouse is old.
- *Letter Book.* Send out a letter to family and friends asking them to write down a memory or something they like about your spouse and send the letters back to you. Compile all the letters into a book. Whenever your spouse is having a bad day, he can read this book and know that he is loved. You might want to send a piece of stationery when you send the letters so each page will have the same size paper.
- *"The Story of Us" Book.* This is a book that you can write together. Start out with "Once upon a time . . ." The first person then writes a paragraph about how you met. The next person continues with

your first date. Continue going until the present and be sure to end with "happily ever after."

- *Date Book.* Write down as many creative dates as you can think of together. You may want to ask each other to write down five dates you would like to go on this year. Include these date ideas in the book. If you are ever having trouble deciding what to do, go to the date book and choose one of the dates.
- *Yearbook.* Make a yearbook for each year you and your spouse have been together, just like your high school yearbook. Divide it in sections: history, songs that mean something, great books read, special dates, quotes, prices of gasoline, candy bars, house payment, and so forth.
- *Picture Book.* Purchase a picture book about love. Change the names in the book to your names and personalize it to fit your relationship.
- *"Oh How I Love You" Book.* Sit down together and write as many things you can think of about why you love your spouse. Compile them into a book with pictures, quotes, and memorabilia. When you are upset with your spouse, pull out the book and remember the things you love about him.

TALK TIME

Sometimes we take for granted that we know everything about our spouse. Sit down with each other and have a talk. Following are some topics to discuss:

- Tell about your favorite game you played as a child.
- Tell about your teenage social life.
- What are your mother's best and worst traits?
- What convinced you most in your choice of spouse?
- What did you want to be when you grew up?
- Describe a favorite vacation.
- Did you have a favorite television show as a child?
- What are you frightened of? Why?
- Describe the perfect day.
- What makes you feel good?
- What is your secret for happiness?
- Tell about your favorite aunt or uncle.
- Tell about any pets you had as a child.

COUNTDOWN TO BIRTHDAY

It is so much fun to build anticipation. The week before your spouse's birthday, give him a little gift to let him know you are thinking of him. Here are some ideas:

- On two slips of paper, write something you love about your spouse. Fold the notes and insert them into deflated balloons. Blow up the balloons and give to your spouse with a pin.
- Make a coupon book for him to use each day the week before his birthday.
- Make a treasure hunt by putting a card in a visible place to start the hunt. Write locations on four hearts along the way, with a love message to lead him to the next clue. End with a special treasure.
- Take his car and wash it inside and out.
- Give him a timer and tell him that you are his for fifteen minutes, interruption free.
- Bake his favorite treat and take it to him at lunchtime.

DVD OF YOUR LIFE TOGETHER

Gather pictures of your life and favorite songs that remind you of each other. Put the pictures in chronological order and make a DVD of your life together.

DINNER FOR TWO

Plan dinner for two on a boat. Rent a rowboat or use one of your own if you have one. Prepare a small dinner complete with candles and take your spouse to the lake. Enjoy the evening floating on the lake under the stars. You may want to pack swimsuits and go for a late-night swim.

STORYBOOK QUILT

Make quilt blocks that depict each year of your life together. You could have the designs screen printed onto the block or piece the blocks together with fabric. This makes a nice anniversary gift.

A GIFT AN HOUR

Give gifts by each hour throughout the day. Start in the morning with breakfast in bed. Then give him a CD of his favorite music. Give gifts to his coworkers to give him throughout the day. Take him out to lunch. This is a fun birthday celebration.

DESSERT

Go to a fancy restaurant and just order dessert.

WISHING WELL

Get a roll of pennies and go to a wishing well. Take turns throwing in pennies and talking about dreams for your future. It gives you great insight into how to make his dreams come true.

FOURTEEN DAYS OF VALENTINES

Countdown to Valentine's Day by giving a note and a treat each day.

- On the first day of Valentine's, I want you to know you are the best. Today you get a foot massage. Sit down and take a rest!
- On the second day of Valentine's, a gift to help you see that somebody really loves you, and that somebody is me. (Purchase some new sunglasses for him.)
- On the third day of Valentine's, to show that you're the real deal, I'm taking you out on the town for your favorite meal. (Give him a gift certificate to his favorite restaurant.)
- On the fourth day of Valentine's, to let you know that you I treasure, my love for you is beyond measure. (Give him a bucket with a measuring tape and other tools that he needs.)
- On the fifth day of Valentine's, it's true I cannot lie. You truly are my sweetie pie. (Make or buy him his favorite pie.)
- On the sixth day of Valentine's, on my list of favorites you are on top. Today to get your message, these balloons you must pop. (Give him a bouquet of balloons with a pin to pop. Put a message in the balloons like, "When it comes to being great, you really take the cake." Tie the balloon bouquet to a cake or some cupcakes.)
- On the seventh day of Valentine's, don't think you've slipped my mind. Today your gift is one that you must find. (Send him on a treasure hunt, ending up with him finding you.)
- On the eighth day of Valentine's, I scream, I scream, you know what I scream? I Love You! (Buy him a gift certificate for his favorite milkshake.)
- On the ninth day of Valentine's, it is my only wish that you will accept and return every hug and kiss. (Give him a bag of hugs and a bag of kisses.)

- On the tenth day of Valentine's, to let you know you're way above the "bar," today you get a detail and cleaning of your car! (Purchase a gift certificate or coupon for a car detailing.)
- On the eleventh day of Valentine's, Cupid's arrow has been shot. A date tonight to let you know that you are loved a lot! (Plan a spectacular date.)
- On the twelfth day of Valentine's, my love for you does not lack. Today you get a shirt to cover up your back! (Give him a shirt that he will love.)
- On the thirteenth day of Valentine's, to be married to you is just ducky. A ticket to watch [his favorite sports team] I hope today will be lucky! (Purchase tickets to go and watch a game together.)
- On the fourteenth day of Valentine's, I want you to know that from the start, you have had the key to my heart. (Include a key to a hotel room for a night's stay.)

SLUMBER PARTY

Have a slumber party in front of the fireplace or the Christmas tree. Or you could sleep out under the stars.

HOMEMADE CALENDAR

Make a calendar and be sure to include all the dates that have special meaning to you. Mark the day you met, your first date, the day you got engaged, and your anniversary.

PICK A PARK

Choose a park that you can call your own. When you want to talk or relax, go to your park!

SPEAK YOUR SPOUSE'S LOVE LANGUAGE

Take a 3x5 card and write down favorite romantic things that your spouse has done for you. Your spouse does the same on his own 3x5 card. Exchange cards and then make a mental note to do more of his favorite things.

SPOUSE SPICE

Fill two jars, one for him and one for her, with fifty-two slips of paper of nice things to do for each other. Draw a slip each week and do what the slip of paper says. See the flavor and spice in your marriage soar!

CREATIVE DATES

- Bake and decorate a gingerbread house together. You could make a haunted house for Halloween, a valentine house for Valentine's Day, and so forth.
- Go on a progressive restaurant date. At the first restaurant order a drink, at the next restaurant get a salad, and continue going to restaurants and ordering one part of the meal. This is a fun way to try out new restaurants.
- Purchase a puzzle and put it together while you talk.
- Fill bags full of useless stuff and make an art project together with the items in the bags.
- Go to an apple orchard and pick apples. Go home and make various apple creations.
- Watch a football or basketball game together. Get lots of snacks, and cheer for your favorite team.

Mealtime Magic

Family Mealtime. . . a Little Taste of Heaven

Life is busy! We try to put family first, but at times it seems we have too many things to do and we will never catch up.

Keeping family together is a struggle. A simple solution for increased family unity is to eat dinner together.

Studies have proven that families who eat dinner together have children with higher self-esteem, better academic performance, and lower use of alcohol and drugs.

Dinner is a perfect time to connect with each other as a family. In this chapter several ideas are given to make dinners convenient, memorable, and fun.

TEN REASONS TO HAVE FAMILY DINNER

1. It is less expensive than eating out and offers fewer distractions from the outside world.
2. You have control of what ingredients are going into the meal.
3. It is a great time to connect with family.
4. It helps teach children the basics of cooking and cleaning.
5. Children will be more likely to communicate their needs with you.
6. Children will get better grades, have higher self-esteem, and are more secure and content.
7. It allows you to let your family know you care.
8. It gives you more time at home.
9. It keeps your family healthy, and lowers risk of obesity.
10. Studies show children want to have family dinnertime.

TEN TIPS FOR ORGANIZING FAMILY DINNER

1. Set a goal to have four to five family dinners a week.
2. Keep it simple; fix your family's favorites.
3. Be prepared by making a list. Shop for one week's worth of recipes at one time.
4. Stock your kitchen with the basics for your favorite recipes.
5. Get the family involved.
6. Find recipes where you can fix and forget, like meals for the slow cooker and freezer meals.
7. Be creative. Present the meals in unique ways. It makes them taste better.
8. On hectic nights order a pizza or get takeout. It still counts if you're together.
9. Make dinnertime fun. Don't discipline at the dinner table. Meal time should provide comfort.
10. Set the mood for the kind of meal you are making.

RULES

You might want to set some rules that every family member should adhere to at dinnertime. For example, no answering the phone, no TV, no iPods, and no other outside distractions. This is family time!

TEN WAYS TO MAKE MEALTIME MORE FUN

- Ditch the dinner table. Who doesn't love a picnic? Have a picnic in your living room.
- Play "Point out the Piggy" to teach etiquette in a fun way. Get a silly picture of a pig. If one person spots another family member using poor manners, they get to say, "You're the piggy!" The offender gets to keep the pig picture until he sees someone else make a manner mistake. Whoever has the piggy at the end of the meal clears the table.
- Make a miniature meal. Serve mini-hamburgers with petite peas, mini-glasses with juice in them. You could even pick a tiny flower and use as a centerpiece.
- Play conversation games, such as "Two Truths and a Lie, using things that happened to you during the day. Everyone else has to guess which one didn't happen.
- Use silly names for new foods. Calling tomatoes "moon-squirters,"

or rice "albino mealy bugs," makes kids want to eat even more.

- Mix up the utensils. Kids eat better and sit longer when eating with different utensils. Use chopsticks, toothpicks, wooden skewers, toy tea set, and other unique utensils to make mealtime more interesting.
- Microwave madness is a great way to use up leftovers. Give each family member sixty seconds to go to the fridge, dish up a plate, and then warm it in the microwave.
- Have each family member be chef for a day. Give the kids the responsibility to plan, shop for, and cook the meal.
- When you try a new recipe, take a vote to see who liked or didn't like the meal. Write the voting results in your cookbook by the new recipe.
- Put a sticker under one person's plate. This sticker is good for a night free from chores.

GET THEM TALKING

- Put a world map on your kitchen table and cover it with a clear plastic tablecloth. When eating dinner, discuss world events. Point out the different countries where news is happening.
- Make a conversation jar. Find an empty mayonnaise or canning jar and cover the lid with fabric. Inside the jar put slips of paper that have conversation starters on them. Pull one conversation starter out at each meal. Every person in the family needs to respond to the slip of paper. Here are some ideas for conversation starters:
  › If you could invite three famous people to dinner, who would they be and why?
  › If I were President . . .
  › If you could have any superpower, which one would you choose?
  › If I could live anywhere . . .
  › If you could be a professional athlete, what sport would you play?
  › A moose is not a good pet because . . .
  › What kind of food do you hate?
  › If you could stop doing one chore around the house, which would it be?

- › If you had to leave the earth on a spaceship and you could take four friends with you, who would you take?
- › What is your favorite smell in the world? Why?
- Ask specific questions about their day. What was your favorite thing you got to do today? Who did you play with at recess? and so forth.
- Rotate nights for joke time. On your night you need to come up with a funny joke to tell at the dinner table.
- Use dinner time to teach an object lesson. Teach a five-minute devotional, using props, and discuss the lesson while you eat. This will stick with them long after you teach it.

GO THE EXTRA MILE
- Set the table in a special way. Use candles, balloons, or candy. Make it look like you really thought about them.
- Write a little note and leave it by each plate.
- Designate a "special plate." The person who sits by that plate gets a compliment from every other family member at mealtime.
- Use a theme. Make a star-shaped meal to celebrate good grades. Make a ball-themed meal when a family member makes a ball team.

CREATIVE COOKING
Present meals in different ways. Some ideas for creative meals are:
- *Tacos to Go.* Use a small bag of Fritos corn chips. Open the bag and add seasoned taco meat, lettuce, cheese, salsa, and sour cream. Shake the bag up and you have a taco to go. Eat with a plastic fork right out of the bag.
- *Omelets in a Bag.* Each person writes his name on a ziplock bag. Crack two eggs in each bag. Have a variety of toppings to add to the eggs, such as ham, cheese, onion, olives, green pepper, and so forth. Each person puts the toppings in the bag and mixes all the ingredients with their hands. Zip the bags shut and put in boiling water for twelve minutes. Pull the bags out, and you have an omelet.
- *Happy Meals.* Make sack lunches for dinner. Put a sandwich, chips, cut-up vegetables, a juice box, and a special treat in each bag.

- *On a Stick.* Everything tastes better when you eat it off a stick. You could make fruit kabobs, vegetable kabobs, meat kabobs, breadsticks on a stick, or hot dogs on a stick (roast them over your stove). Make dinner a fondue party. Give each person a kabob stick to dip whatever he wants. Make salad on a stick by putting rolled up lettuce, cut-up cucumbers, cherry tomatoes, cookie-cutter cut cheese, carrots, and olives on a stick and then dip in salad dressing.
- *Wrap it up.* Make tinfoil dinners by layering a hamburger patty, sliced potatoes, carrots, and onions. Sprinkle salt and pepper on top. Wrap in tinfoil and bake for 35–45 minutes in a 350 degree oven.
- *Dippers.* Make foods that you can dip into a sauce, such as chicken strips, french toast sticks, cut-up vegetables, corn dogs, french fries, fruit, or quesadillas.
- *Fancy Goblets.* Serve salads in fancy goblets instead of on plates. Make parfaits in clear goblets—they look irresistible.
- *Cookie Cutters.* Make shapes out of food. It is amazing how fast kids eat cheese or meat that has been cut into shapes.
- *Funny Faces.* Use fruit or vegetables to make funny faces on top of food. Sandwiches, pizzas, casseroles, and soups are some things on which you can add a funny face to add a little extra to the meal.
- *Ice Cream Cones.* Serve a snack mix in ice cream cones, or fill the cone with fruit.

HOLIDAY COOKING

Before each holiday, plan meals that go with the holiday theme. Building anticipation for a holiday is just as much fun as the celebration itself. The following ideas will help you throughout the year.

- *New Year's Day.* Serve a deluxe breakfast. Make an assortment of appetizers. Build your own bar, such as a potato bar, salad bar, taco bar, Hawaiian haystacks bar, or sandwich bar. This will allow each person to get exactly what they want, and your day will be complaint-free.
- *Chinese New Year.* Celebrate the start of the Chinese New Year by eating Chinese food. Learn your fortune with the zodiac calendar, and learn to fold origami.

- *Valentine's Day.* Make a red meal. Some ideas might include spaghetti with marinara sauce, breadsticks dyed pink, and salad with red peppers and radishes on it. Serve cherry cheesecake for dessert. You could also have a heart-shaped meal for Valentine's Day. Make heart-shaped pizza or sandwiches, sugar cookies, or heart-shaped ice to put in the drink. Valentine's Day is a good time for candlelight at dinner.

- *St. Patrick's Day.* Serve corned beef and cabbage, irish soda bread or irish stew. You could also make a green meal. Serve green salad, green mashed potatoes, spinach spiral steak, green jell-o, and pistachio cake (yellow cake mix: add a small box of instant pistachio pudding). Another fun St. Patrick's day meal is a rainbow meal. Make something that is each color of the rainbow and have a pot of gold at the end of the rainbow. A fun recipe for "gold" is miniature peanut butter Ritz crackers dipped in melted butterscotch chips.

- *April Fool's Day.* Each year I make a meal that fools my family.
  › Make meatloaf cupcakes. Make meatloaf and put one half cup of mixture in a silver cupcake liner. Bake as you would meatloaf, top with mashed potatoes (dyed pink) to look like frosting. I make regular cupcakes too and serve them first.
  › Ice cream and caramel topping make great fake mashed potatoes and gravy.
  › Coconut covered marshmallows, or sliced bananas rolled in crushed vanilla wafers look just like chicken nuggets.
  › Pound cake sliced and toasted in the toaster and then filled with orange frosting looks like a grilled cheese sandwich.
  › Marshmallow topping filled with a scoop of lemon pudding looks like a fried egg.

- *Easter.* Set the table with a nest setting. Sprinkle Easter grass on the table under the plate. Place settings could be made with hard boiled eggs that have been dyed. Write each person's name on the egg and set one by each plate. A traditional meal of ham, potato salad, scalloped potatoes, rolls, and cake could be served. You could also use a bunny theme. Make bunny-shaped sandwiches using cookie cutters. Serve bunny pear salad (half of a canned pear for face, raisins for eyes, carrot slices for whiskers). Eat Nutter Butter cookies dipped in white chocolate with paper ears for dessert. An egg-themed meal is also fun. Make egg salad sandwiches or deviled eggs, potato salad, and egg-shaped jell-o. Or, prepare eggs in different ways, such as scrambled, fried, poached, or boiled.

- *Mother's Day.* Make a Mother's Day brunch with a breakfast casserole, sweet rolls, juice, and fruit. Let the kids make mom breakfast in bed. Also, fruit and yogurt parfaits are easy and impressive.
- *Father's Day.* Have a barbecue. Grill hamburgers, hot dogs, steaks, or chicken. Serve with corn on the cob, scalloped potatoes, and pie.
- *Fourth of July.* The Fourth of July is a great day for all Americans to celebrate the birth of America. This was the day the Declaration of Independence was signed and America officially became a free country. Make a patriotic meal, serving only red, white, and blue food. You could have a strawberry, blueberry, and yogurt salad. Sloppy joes or hamburgers on white buns, star-shaped crackers, and vegetables also make great Fourth of July food. Serve old-fashioned apple pie for dessert.
- *Halloween.* Make a meal that nobody will forget. Start off with a menu that has things like witches fingers (breadsticks), bat's blood (spaghetti sauce), ghostly grub (spaghetti noodles), slime (salad), and so forth. Give each person a pencil and have them pick three items. You should serve this meal in three courses. Think of twelve to fifteen items to put on the menu.
- *Thanksgiving.* Serve a traditional Thanksgiving meal of turkey, mashed potatoes and gravy, stuffing, salads, and pie. Or, you could make a list of foods that your family is thankful for and have a gratitude dinner with the foods that each family member chooses.
- *Christmas.* Make a dinner with the symbols of Christmas as your theme.
  - › The evergreen tree symbolizes everlasting life. (Make a vegetable tree made with a styrofoam cone. Use toothpicks to adhere vegetables like broccoli, lettuce, carrots, tomatoes, and olives to the cone.)
  - › Stars symbolize the light of Christ. (Make star-shaped sandwiches.)

> › The yule log symbolizes the fire of the spirit. (Serve pretzel rods.)
>
> › Sheep symbolize the good shepherd. (Serve ice cream balls to make the sheep bodies, and use tootsie rolls for the legs and the head.)
>
> › A manger filled with hay symbolizes Jesus' humility. (Serve shredded wheat to look like hay.)
>
> › Candy canes symbolize the shepherd's crook used to gather his sheep. (Make hot chocolate, with a candy cane to stir it.)

- Learn about different holidays around the world and prepare meals for these holidays. This will teach your family about new traditions and give them a taste from around the world.

GETTING HELP

It is very difficult to plan, cook, clean, shop, and carry out mealtime if you do it alone. I am a firm believer that everyone should contribute to family mealtime. Here are some ideas for getting your family to happily help you with mealtime.

- Let each family member choose a meal that they would like to eat each week.
- Divide up the cooking. One person is in charge of the main dish, one in charge of salad, one in charge of bread, and one in charge of dessert. Rotate responsibilities so everyone has a chance to do everything.
- Divide up the cleaning tasks. One person clears the table, one wipes the table and countertops, one sweeps the floor, and one does the dishes. Rotate the chores through each member of the family.
- Let a child set the table and allow them to set it the way they want. I have kids who like to make place settings. Some of them throw the dishes on the table and we have to find our own setting, while some set it fancy like at a restaurant by folding the napkins and setting out the fancy china. It is good experience for them to learn how to set a table.
- When planning meals for the week, have the children look up the recipes and make sure that all the groceries are on the shopping list or already in the pantry.
- Give each person in the family a night to cook dinner. They get

to plan what to cook. At the first of the week they should have a list of groceries needed for their meal.

- Each person in the family could have a night to clean the kitchen. One night a week if possible.
- Put four to five ingredients in a paper bag. Let each family member choose an item out of the bag. They will need to make their part of dinner with this ingredient. You are sure to get some unique meals this way!

HELPFUL HINTS ON PLANNING

- Half the battle is deciding what to cook. Make a menu for the week, purchase the groceries for the menu, and then keep the menu in sight so you will know what to cook.
- Prepare ahead as much as you can. Get meat out of the freezer the night before so it can defrost in the fridge. Chop up vegetables and grate cheese ahead of time. Set the table in the morning when you can. These helpful hints save time in the evening.
- When making a casserole, make two and put one in the freezer. Pull the freezer meal out on a busy day of the week.
- Cook meals in a slow cooker. They can slow cook all day and the aroma will entice your children into the kitchen when they get home.
- Stock your kitchen with basic spices and ingredients so you don't have to run to the store when you get ready to cook.
- Look at your schedule for the day. If you know you won't have a lot of time to cook, plan a meal that takes very little time to prepare.
- Enlist your family in helping you plan. If they take part in the planning, they are more likely to enjoy the meals.

UNIQUE MEALS

- *Leftover Restaurant.* Make a menu of all the leftovers in your fridge. Pass the menu to your family and then go to them like a waitress and ask for their order. This is a great way to use up leftovers!
- *Crazy Cuisine.* Serve a dinner where you assign crazy names to the food, utensils, and dinnerware. Each person can only choose five items and must eat on what is given to them. Each person

can earn more items by doing a quick chore or performing some other task. It's crazy, but they keep asking to do it over and over again.

- *Iron Chef Challenge.* Divide into two teams. The task is to create an appetizer, main dish, or dessert while using a secret ingredient. The secret ingredient is given to them in a brown paper bag, which they are not to open until they begin. Give them a time limit. Meet back together after the time is up and share your creations with the other team.

- *Progressive Dinner.* Start in one room with an appetizer. Go to the next room for salad and drink. The next room could serve the main dish and side dish, and the last room could serve dessert. Each person is in charge of one of the courses of the meal.

- *Treasure Hunt.* Send your family on a treasure hunt to get all the ingredients for dinner. Come back, cook the meal, and enjoy your treasure!

- *Picnic in the House.* Spread out a blanket and have a picnic inside.

- *Go OUT to Dinner.* Tell your family you are going out to dinner. When everyone is in the car, drive around for a while. Stop at a park where you have a table set, nice music playing, and candles ready to be lit. Explain that their meal will soon be delivered. Arrange with a friend to deliver dinner to you: one course at a time every ten minutes. Or, call and have pizza delivered.

- *Blindfolded Dinner.* Have everyone guess what ingredients you put in the food. The family member who guesses the most ingredients correctly gets dessert first.

- *Backwards Meal.* Serve dessert first. Set the chairs up at the table backwards. Everyone must turn their shirt around so it is backwards.

FIFTEEN-MINUTE MEALS

You can't even get pizza or Chinese takeout delivered in fifteen minutes. Try out some of these fifteen-minute meals when you are in a time crunch.

- *Tacos.* Brown hamburger, and cut up lettuce, tomato, and olives. Set out taco shells, tortillas, and salsa. Have everyone make their own taco.

- *Pizza Soup.* In a microwave-safe bowl, mix 1 package dry chicken noodle soup, 3 cups water, 1 jar pizza sauce, 1 fifteen-ounce can italian style tomatoes, and 3 ounces pepperoni. Microwave for twelve minutes. Top with grated cheese and croutons.

- *Malibu Chicken.* Top precooked chicken patties with thinly sliced ham and swiss cheese. Bake at 350 degrees for 10 minutes. Serve with a mustard and mayonnaise sauce.
- *Paninis.* Top bread with lunch meat and cheese of choice. Cook on a grill or in a panini oven for five minutes. Add chopped vegetables of choice.
- *French Dip Sandwiches.* Heat thinly sliced roast beef in au jus, and put on top of hoagie buns. Serve with cut-up vegetables.
- *Stir Fry.* Stir fry cut-up chicken breast until browned. Add cut up vegetables such as broccoli, carrots, peppers, and snap peas. Top with your favorite teriyaki sauce and rice.
- *Spaghetti.* Boil spaghetti noodles. In separate pan, brown hamburger and top with one jar of spaghetti sauce. Drain noodles and top with sauce. Serve with salad.
- *Sloppy Joes.* Brown hamburger, and add 1 can chicken gumbo soup, 1 cup ketchup, and 1 tablespoon mustard. Simmer for five minutes. Put meat and pickles on top of hamburger buns.
- *Chicken Pot Pie.* You will need 2 premade pie crusts, 2 cans chicken pot pie soup, and 1 package frozen mixed vegetables. Put one pie crust in a pie baking dish and add soup and vegetables. Top with other pie crust. Bake at 375 degrees for 15 minutes.
- *Pigs in a Blanket.* Wrap hot dogs in crescent dinner rolls. Bake 375 degrees for 10–12 minutes. Dip in ketchup and mustard.
- *Egg McMuffins.* Toast english muffins. Scramble eggs and put on one muffin. Top with sliced ham and cheddar cheese. Put the other muffin on top and serve with your favorite fruit smoothie.
- *Easiest Ever Enchiladas.* You will need 1 can chunk chicken, 1 can diced green chilies, tortillas, grated cheese, and 2 cans cream of chicken soup. Mix chicken, chilies, and 1 can of soup together. Scoop ½ cup of chicken mixture in a tortilla. Roll tightly and place in baking dish. Continue until mixture is gone. Top enchiladas with other can of soup and grated cheese. Bake 350 degrees for 10–15 minutes, or until warmed through.
- *Ham Dinner.* Lay sliced ham on a baking sheet. Top with pineapple chunks and brown sugar. Broil for 5 minutes. Serve

with potatoes or rice.

- *Alfredo.* Boil linguine noodles and drain. Heat up a bottle of alfredo sauce and pour sauce over noodles. Steam vegetables and put on top of sauce. Sprinkle with parmesan cheese.
- *Grilled Hamburgers.* Make hamburger patties, seasoned as desired. Grill for 5 minutes on each side, and top with cheese. Cut up lettuce, pickles, and tomatoes. Set out ketchup and mustard.

FIX AND FORGET MEALS

Slow-cooker cooking is an excellent option for having a home cooked meal. Just throw the ingredients in the slow cooker in the morning and dinner will be ready when everyone gets home in the evening. Some great meals in the slow cooker are pot roast, roasted chicken, barbecue spare-ribs, turkey breast, beef stew, and chicken noodle soup. The following are tips for great slow cooker meals.

- Buy a slow cooker that has a removable stoneware liner. This makes cleanup a breeze. Do not wash the liner in the dishwasher or store it in the fridge. That will make the cooking temperature in the liner change.
- When cooking in a slow cooker only fill one-half to two-thirds full. The food will not cook properly if the slow cooker is too full.
- You can buy less expensive cuts of meat when cooking in a slow cooker. The slow cooking process makes any meat tender.
- Always brown ground meats in another pan before placing in the slow cooker.
- Add spices and seasonings during the last half of cooking to ensure ultimate flavor.

MONTHLY COOKING

Write down a menu for the month. Spend one full day cooking and end up with a month's worth of meals.

Cook your meat at the same time. Chop all the vegetables and grate the cheese. Start assembling your meals. Place them in ziplock bags or casserole dishes. Label your meals well with the proper cooking instructions, and you won't have to think about cooking for another month. Lasagna, enchiladas, meatballs, and baked chicken all freeze well.

NEIGHBORHOOD COOKING GROUP

Get together with some neighbors and friends that have families about the same size as yours. You cook for these families one night and they cook for you on another. This way you only cook once or twice a week and yet you have good nutritious meals all week long. This method saves time and money. As a group, plan menus that every family likes. Evaluate the menus at your next planning meeting.

CULTURE MEALS

Get an education while eating dinner. Teaching your children about different cultures is fun and memorable when you use a meal to establish a "taste" of other cultures's traditions. You can use these ideas anytime, but there are holidays we celebrate for just about every culture. Eating a meal from a certain culture and teaching children the purpose for that particular holiday makes these meals more meaningful and memorable. Learn about different cultures and expand your horizons.

Island Luau

Make tickets and hand them out the night before the dinner. On the tickets write your destination: Hawaii. Play Hawaiian music, and do the limbo. Serve Hawaiian haystacks (rice, chicken, gravy, pineapple, celery, tomatoes, grated carrots, almonds, and coconut). Let each person make their own haystack. You could also make kalua pork, fruit kabobs, and piña coladas.

Cinco De Mayo Mexican Fiesta

Prepare a Mexican meal, serving enchiladas, tamales, burritos, or tacos. Have chips and salsa on the side. Serve Nacho Dulce for dessert (baked or deep fried flour tortillas topped with vanilla ice cream, honey butter and cinnamon). Discuss Mexican culture, break a piñata, decorate with sombreros, or play Spanish match game, where you match Spanish words and their English equivalent.

Oriental Night

Eat dinner on the floor. Make egg drop soup, stir fry, and rice. Eat your dinner with chopsticks and learn how to fold origami. Don't forget the fortune cookies!

Italian Feast

Decorate with red, green, and white. Serve spaghetti, lasagna, manicotti, pizza, or have a pasta bar. Play Italian music while you eat. End the meal with Italian ice or spumoni ice cream.

Mardi Gras

The biggest party of them all is in New Orleans and is called Mardi Gras. Study up on some of the traditions of Mardi Gras and make some jambalaya.

Tex Mex Barbecue

Everything is bigger in Texas! Prepare a meal of barbecue spareribs, dutch oven potatoes, salads, and brownie sundaes. Square dance or line dance.

Greece

Serve souvlaki, gyros, yellow rice, and baklava. Instruct each family member to come prepared with a new fact about Greece. Hold a family olympics, since Greece was the first country to host the olympics.

Germany

Have your own Oktoberfest! Serve bratwurst, sauerkraut, pretzels, and root beer. Each family member could learn a new word in German and teach their word to the rest of the family.

France

Serve crepes, au gratin potatoes, cheese and crackers, pancakes, and streusel. Watch a movie that is filmed in France. Speak with a French accent.

Carnival in Spain

Spain celebrates carnival the week before Lent. Have the girls dress up in fancy dresses like Flamenco dancers. Serve paella, spanish bread, and flan.

DINNER PARTIES

Invite other families to dinner and teach your children social skills. This is a good opportunity to see how your children relate to other adults and children, while having fun!

- Guess who's coming to dinner! Host a party and invite a family in your neighborhood. Don't let your family know who's coming.
- Host a health and wellness night. Set your house up like a spa, and serve healthy food.
- Have a two-dollar night. Hand out two dollars and a slips of paper that say vegetable, drink, main dish, appetizer, side dish, and dessert. Each person in your family picks a paper and has

to buy all the ingredients for his part of the meal with the two dollars. Everyone comes home and prepares the meal together.

- Enjoy a boxed dinner. Each person makes a dinner and puts it in a box with a number on it. Put all the numbers in a bowl and draw a number. That will determine which meal each person gets for dinner.

- Have a tacky party. Invite your family to dinner with used envelopes. Make bologna sandwiches on hard bread. Dress and act tacky.

- Compete in a cook off! Each person gets a paper bag with a secret ingredient and a food assignment. Everyone will have to incorporate their secret ingredient into what they prepare.

- Relive your past with a decade party. Each family member chooses a decade from the past and plans a meal around it. You could do a diner meal for the 1950s, a USO club for the 1940s, dress as hippies for the 1960s, and have a disco theme for the 1970s.

- Invite your neighbors over for a block party. Have everyone bring their own meat to barbecue and a potluck dish such as a salad or dessert.

- Go on a "Bike-A-Meal-Scavenger Hunt." Get on your bikes and go find your meal. Have someone at each stop with a part of your meal. When you get the whole meal together, sit down and have a picnic.

- Go on a cruise for dinner! Set your house up like a cruise ship. Make a buffet for the meal, and learn magic tricks and entertain during dinner.

- Find out who did it with a murder mystery dinner. There are numerous murder mystery games you can purchase. Each person acts out their part and everyone works to solve the mystery over dinner.

Traditions That Build Unity

Traditions Hold us Together and Build Unity

Traditions reinforce connections with your family. Each time a tradition is carried out, you build a stronger relationship. Traditions are like the thread that binds together patches of a quilt. Studies show that if a child can name multiple family traditions, that child is more likely to have positive feelings about his family life.

Each family is unique and must create its own traditions. In this chapter, many ideas are provided to help you start or add to your own traditions. Make a goal to add a new family tradition this year!

TRADITIONS FOR JANUARY

Calendar Night

Give each person in your family a calendar on the first of January. Sit down together and fill in your calendars. Mark birthdays and other special days, schedule a family vacation, mark one-on-one parent-child time, and plan family night. Write your family traditions down to give you something to look forward to and plan for.

New Year's Tree

Decorate the Christmas tree with noisemakers, confetti, sparklers to light outside at midnight, and add paper streamers. Blow up balloons with notes inside of them. (The notes could say things like choose a game and play it now, treat time, and so forth.) Each hour, pop a balloon and do what the note says.

Quarter for Luck

Wrap a quarter in aluminum foil and bake it into a cake. Cut the cake on New Year's Eve. The person who gets the quarter will be extra lucky in the coming year.

Predictions

Give each person a paper and have them write down three things they think will happen in the coming year. Put them in a jar to keep for the next year. Open up the jar from the previous year and read the predictions. It is great to see what things happened and what did not.

Rehang Your Stockings

Hang your Christmas stockings up again for a refill. Fill the stockings with supplies needed for the next year. It is a good time to re-stock the school supplies, shampoo, soap, toothpaste, and so forth.

Midnight Madness

In the winter months the sky is clear and the stars are very bright. Go on a midnight walk, cross-country ski, star gaze, or snowmobile ride. Come back inside and have breakfast at midnight.

Super Swap

Each person in the family gathers ten to fifteen unwanted items. Put all the items on the kitchen table. Each person in the family can come and choose five items that they want from the pile. The rest of the items can be given to a charity.

TRADITIONS FOR FEBRUARY

Mailboxes

Purchase a small mailbox for each member of the family, or use small boxes. Everyone decorates his own mailbox and puts his mailbox in his room. Deliver notes, treats, surprises etc. to family members. When you put an item in the mailbox, put the flag up. When the flag is up that person will know that he has mail.

Heart Attacks

Cut out hearts from different colored paper. Write notes on each of the hearts. Tape the hearts to doors, pillows, shower curtains, or the car windshield. One of the hearts should say, "You just had a heart attack. We love you!"

Perfect Presents

On Valentine's Day, Dad delivers roses to his girls and Mom delivers sugar cookies to her boys.

Bit By the Lovebug

February is a great time to let others know you care. Each week during the month of February pass on the lovebug bite.

- First week: Write two letters to people you are thankful for. Be sure to let them know why you chose to write to them.
- Second week: Make three phone calls, just to chat.
- Third week: Bake a batch of cookies and deliver them to a family.
- Fourth week: Pray for someone. Think of ways you can be an answer to someone's prayers.

Everyone Gets a Valentine

Order 4 dozen helium filled balloons and make 4 dozen cookies. Attach the cookies to the balloons. Deliver the balloons and cookies to people who you think might not get a Valentine. It is very rewarding to see the smiles on their faces.

Anonymous Valentines

Start a tradition by sending an anonymous Valentine to someone.

Valentine Placemats

Take all the little valentines your child receives and glue them onto a paper the size of a placemat. Laminate and then use for a few weeks after Valentines.

Superbowl Party

Serve soup out of football shaped bread bowls, or make pigskin potato bar. Decorate with the colors of the football teams. Make guesses on the score of the game, who will win, and what commercial is going to be the big hit. Enjoy the football game while snacking a variety of treats.

TRADITIONS FOR MARCH

SOS

Seek Out Service. Be on the lookout for service you can do as a family. Shovel someone's sidewalk, feed your neighbor's pets when they are gone on vacation, walk around the block and pick up garbage, clean your church, visit a rest home, help with special Olympics, help serve dinner at a homeless shelter, or volunteer at the hospital. Carry out these service projects together. A great family tradition!

Kid's Day

Wake your kids up to their favorite breakfast in bed. Give them a break from their chores for a day! Take them on a string treasure hunt where they must follow a string around the house to get to a present at the end. Spotlight each child by telling the story of his birth, letting each child know you are grateful for him. Make a candlelight dinner and play games together. This is the kids' day!

March Forth

March fourth is the only day that is a command! Parade around the house to a marching song, write down a goal for the year, read off the goals from the previous year, and have a prize for the person who best accomplished his goals.

Luck of the Irish

During the month of March, hide a lucky shamrock around your house. The person who finds the shamrock that day gets a quarter.

Leprechaun Visit

The night before St. Patrick's Day, sprinkle gold candies (Rolos, gold coins, butterscotch candies) on the floor around your child's bed. Stamp little leprechaun footprints with washable green paint on the counter in the bathroom or kitchen. The kids will look forward to the leprechaun visit each year.

Green Basket Knock-and-Run

Think of someone in your neighborhood to deliver a basket full of green items to. You can give items such as green spices, green fruit or vegetables, green dinnerware, or a potted plant. Attach a note that says, "We are lucky to have you as friends." Sneak up to their front porch and leave the basket. Knock on the door and run. Make sure you don't get caught!

Favorite Teacher Dinner

Each person in your family chooses his favorite teacher. Make invitations and invite the teachers to your home for dinner. The person who nominates each teacher should write a thank you letter to his teacher saying why he chose him as his favorite teacher.

TRADITIONS FOR APRIL

April Fool's Day Pranks

You can't let April first go by without doing a few good-natured pranks. Mix up the meals. Serve dinner for breakfast and breakfast for dinner. Sew up the fly on dad's underwear. Unscrew the shower head and fill it with a package of red kool-aid; when the shower turns on that person will get a big surprise! The night before when the kids are sound asleep, sneak into their rooms and carefully lift them out of bed and switch bedrooms with them. When they wake up they won't know how in the world they got into their brother's or sister's rooms.

The Hunt

Hold an annual Easter egg hunt. Hide eggs around your yard, numbering some of them. The kids who find the numbered eggs come to the "prize store" and cash in their egg for a prize.

True Meaning of Easter Eggs

Fill twelve plastic eggs with scriptures or items to represent the verses that tell the Easter story. Leave the twelfth egg empty. Number the eggs and hide them around your home. When all twelve eggs are found, open them up one by one, read the scripture, and discuss the Easter story. When you get to the twelfth egg, which is empty, talk about how the tomb was also empty.

Easter Basket Fillers

Fill a basket with plastic eggs. Inside each egg place a coupon for time spent together, a new book, or a night out for ice cream. Be creative and include things you know your children will love.

Easter Egg Hunt Ideas

- Sprinkle candy around and give each child a basket to go and collect the candy.
- Have a color-coded egg hunt. Each child picks a color out of a hat. When they go searching for eggs they can only pick up eggs of their color.
- Make the egg hunt a treasure hunt also. Inside the eggs, place clues to find the next egg. The clues should lead them to a treasure.
- Hide one egg that is a "golden egg." The person who finds that egg gets a ten dollar bill.

TRADITIONS FOR MAY

Basket Giveaway

Fill a large basket full with treats, groceries for dinner, lotions, soaps, and other assorted items. Deliver the basket to someone who needs it.

Flowers for All
Pick bunches of wild flowers and arrange them into bouquets. Go to the cemetery and place the flowers on the graves.

Cemetery Scavenger Hunt
Prepare a list of information that your children will need to find while walking through the cemetery. For example, find someone who died while fighting in a war, find someone who died before they were one year old, or find someone who is a relative of our family. This is a great way to get them interested in their ancestors and those who came before.

Boat Float
In the spring when the streams are running, it is a great time to hold a boat float. Each person in the family makes his own boat. Once the boats are made, walk to a nearby stream and launch your boats. (Be sure to look for smaller, slower running streams.) Follow the boats down the stream. The boat that makes it to the end first is the winner. Return home and have banana split boats for a treat.

Mom's the Word
Make an ABC book for Mom. Purchase a blank notebook and cut out pictures from magazines that remind you of Mom. Continue until you have made a page for each letter of the alphabet!

Thankful to Be Mom
On Mother's Day, the mom could write cards to each of her kids letting them know how thankful she is to be their mom.

TRADITIONS FOR JUNE

School's Out Party
The day school gets out, greet your children at the bus stop with ice cream cones. They can share the ice cream cones with their friends and celebrate the official start of summer.

Drive-in Movie
Set up a projector in your backyard. Sew four white sheets together and hang them on the back of your home. Pick out a good movie and invite neighbors and friends to come watch an outdoor movie. Have everyone bring their own lawn chairs and blankets. Fill a table with a variety

of movie treats. Start the movie when it gets dark. You could schedule a drive-in movie each month in the summer.

King for a Day

On Father's Day, make Dad king for a day. Make him a deluxe breakfast in bed, do all his chores for him, and provide him with everything he needs to do his favorite activity. Continue the celebration with a barbecue for dinner.

Dad's Detail

Mom and the kids could detail dad's car for Father's Day. Give it a good cleaning inside and out. Load the car with a new air freshener and a new CD. Leave a note on the steering wheel thanking him for everything he does for the family.

TRADITIONS FOR JULY

Patriotic Trivia

In the weeks leading up to the Fourth of July, teach your children various patriotic facts. You could teach them how our country began, who signed the Declaration of Independence, who was the first President, and information about famous people of that time period.

Afterwards, play a trivia game. Give a prize to the person who answers the most questions correctly.

Fireworks

Scope out a good fireworks show in your area; pack your favorite treats, grab your blankets and some games to play while you wait, and enjoy celebrating our country's birthday with your family.

Snowman in July

This tradition is one that you have to think of in the winter. When there is snow, make a miniature snowman. Wrap the snowman in plastic wrap and put him in the freezer. On the fourth of July, pull the snowman out and put him out in your yard. Have each person in the family guess how long it will take for the snowman to melt. The person with the closest guess gets a prize.

Decorate Your Bikes

Decorate your bikes with red, white, and blue crepe paper, helium filled balloons, and American flags. Ride them up and down the street and say "Happy Birthday America." You could even throw candy to the neighbors!

TRADITIONS FOR AUGUST AND SEPTEMBER

Family Olympics

This is a good tradition to do with your extended family. Set up an olympic course. Make T-shirts to represent your family. Olympic events could include a three-legged race, watermelon seed spitting contest, water balloon toss, water balloon volleyball, pie eating contest, wheelbarrow race, bubble blowing contest, and a rubber duck race in a child's swimming pool. Time the events and award everyone with medals.

True Treasure Hunt

When you are on a beach vacation, fill a treasure chest will different prizes. Bury the treasure chest in the sand and cover it with brush. Draw a map that leads to the treasure. You could even burn the edges of the map to make it look like a real pirate map. Sprinkle coins along the way and let the children go on a true treasure hunt.

Yearly Vacation

Schedule a yearly family vacation. If you go to the same place each year, carry out the same traditions year after year at that spot. If you go to different places each year, take some time each year to learn about the place you will be going to. Talk about the things you will do and build the anticipation of a great adventure. Vacations are wonderful tradition builders and memory makers!

Back to School

The week before school starts, plan a dinner that resembles a school lunch. Purchase lunch trays, and serve school lunch food such as chicken nuggets, canned peaches, carrot and celery sticks, cookies, and cartons of milk. Play games where the kids can earn school supplies as prizes.

TRADITIONS FOR OCTOBER

Halloween Fun

- Dress up as a witch and scare the children who come trick-or-treating.
- Make the kids perform a trick to get a treat.
- Sit out on your front porch dressed as a scarecrow. When the kids ring the bell, say "Boo!"

Drop in for Doughnuts

Start a tradition of making homemade doughnuts and apple cider.

Invite the neighborhood over to celebrate with you.

Phantom Neighborhood Ghost

Write a poem that says to pass a treat and a picture of a ghost to another neighbor. Pretty soon the whole neighborhood will be visited by the phantom.

Pumpkin Carving Night

Have each person carve a pumpkin and then light the jack-o-lanterns on your porch the week before Halloween. Roast the pumpkin seeds from the pumpkin, and share with neighbors for a fun Halloween treat.

Costume Party and Contest

Give each member of your family an invitation to a costume party. Each person is in charge of rounding up their own costume. The night of the party have a contest and give prizes for the most creative, the scariest, the most unique, and the funniest costume.

TRADITIONS FOR NOVEMBER

Gratitude Night

Write notes to people you are grateful for. Start a gratitude journal where each day you write things you are thankful for. Express gratitude to each member of your family. Put five kernels of corn by each person's plate, and take turns having each person tell five things they are most grateful for.

ABCs of Gratitude

Each person gets a paper with the ABCs and his name written on it. Start passing the papers around, write something nice about the person whose paper you have that starts with the letter A. Continue passing papers and going through the alphabet. Give each person their paper so they can read all the nice things the family has written.

Thanksgiving Tablecloth

Purchase a cloth tablecloth and some fabric markers. Everyone signs his name, writes what they are most grateful for, and writes the year on the tablecloth. Use this tablecloth year after year. It is fun to see who was at Thanksgiving dinner and what they were grateful for. A gratitude journal could also be passed around and kept year after year.

Pie Night

The Saturday or Sunday before Thanksgiving invite the extended family over for pie night. Each person makes their favorite pie and brings it to share. Don't fix a meal, just have pie!

Thankful Blessing Mix

Make a big bowl of snack mix made up of Bugles (cornucopias), cranberries (symbol of the harvest), pretzels (arms folded in prayer), candy corn (represents the five kernels of corn the pilgrims were given to eat the first year they were here), and sunflower seeds (bounteous harvest). Mix together and put in small bags. Take the blessing mix to neighbors and friends with a note telling them they are a blessing in your life.

Fall Foliage

Go for a hike or a drive and enjoy the fall colors. Pack a picnic lunch or have a fireside cookout. Take a camera along and get some candid photos. Rake the leaves into a pile and jump into them. Enjoy nature and the autumn season before it is too late.

TRADITIONS FOR DECEMBER

Christmas Wish List

On Thanksgiving night have everyone write his Christmas wish list and place it in a shoe left outside the door. Take the list and replace it with a trinket.

Story-A-Day Until Christmas

Gather twenty-four Christmas books and wrap them in Christmas paper. Each night before bed open one book and read it. Continue this tradition each night until Christmas.

Secret Service Elf

Make a card that says, "SSE (secret service elf) has been here because you are loved. When you receive the SSE card you must perform a secret act of service for someone else and leave the card for them to pass on." Some ideas for acts of service:

- Make someone's bed.
- Clean up a mess without being asked.
- Unload the dishwasher.
- Leave a treat on someone's pillow.
- Sweep or vacuum the floor.

- Read a story to a brother or sister.
- Practice music or do homework without being asked.

Culture Night

During the holiday season, attend a play or concert. Purchase tickets and make this an event everyone will look forward to.

Ultimate Party

On Christmas Eve get the extended family together. Eat appetizers and finger foods, break a piñata, and play games. Draw names beforehand and have a gift exchange. Act out the Nativity, and celebrate the season.

Advent Calendar

Counting down the days until Christmas is a fun way to build anticipation. Make a calendar that has little envelopes on it, and in each envelope, write down an activity to do that day. You could decorate cookies, deliver gifts to neighbors, play a game, attend a play, go caroling, make and decorate a gingerbread house, write Christmas cards, go shopping, or wrap presents.

You could also make a paper chain and write the activities on the chain or hang twenty-four little stockings and put the items in the socks. Instead of activities to do, you could include treats for them to find each day.

Live Nativity

Gather costumes and have each member of the family dress up as someone in the Nativity. If available, go to a barn where there are sheep, donkeys, and cows, and act out the Nativity there.

Talent Show

Each year on Christmas Eve, my children put on a play that they have written for us. They send out invitations, make refreshments, and dress up in costumes. This has become a tradition that we really look forward to. One year they all dressed up as snowmen with sheets and pillows. They even had carrots for noses! They also played a song on the piano and we sang Christmas carols together.

Cookie Exchange

Invite your neighbors to a cookie exchange. Each family brings four dozen of their favorite cookies. Exchange cookies so each family will go home with four dozen cookies. The variety of cookies is fun, and you don't have to do all the baking.

New Ornament

Think back over the past year and purchase an ornament that represents the year. Did you go on a fun family vacation? Did someone graduate? Was there a big birthday? Did your favorite sports team do well? These are just a few ideas to work with. Pick something that will be special to your family.

All Decked Out

Fill a basket with homemade bread, jam, butter and a knife. Make a card that says, "We voted your house the best decorated this year." Drive around the neighborhood and look at all the Christmas lights. Vote on which house you like best and secretly deliver the basket to that family.

BIRTHDAY TRADITIONS

Birthday Buzz

Decorate the birthday kid's room with balloons and posters. Celebrate the big day for the whole week. Invite Grandpa and Grandma for dinner the Sunday before. Invite friends over to have a party. Let the birthday kid choose an activity for the whole family to do.

Aunt and Uncle Spoil Day

On birthdays the aunts and uncles take the birthday kid shopping. They have a set amount of money they can spend and let the birthday kid choose what stores to go in and what to buy. Take them to lunch at a nice restaurant let them order whatever they want. Don't forget dessert!

Birthday Dinner

Allow the birthday kid to decide what to have for dinner and invite extended family over. Go around the table, and have each person state his favorite thing about the birthday kid. Let the birthday kid know how special he is to you.

MISCELLANEOUS TRADITONS

Daily Devotionals

Take fifteen minutes in the morning to have a little devotional. Read the scriptures, say a family prayer, tell an inspiring story, or teach a lesson. This fifteen minutes together in the morning will help everyone's day go better.

Monthly Family Time

Once a month get the extended family together for dinner. Catch up on what's happening in everyone's lives. Play games and have fun together.

Worship Together

Make church a weekly tradition in your family. Attend your church services together and discuss what everyone learned. Serve in your church and your community as a family. Pray together. Reach beyond self-help, to spiritual help. Research shows that worshipping together is one of the major characteristics of healthy, happy families.

Work Together

Plant a garden, clean the house, mow the lawn, shovel the sidewalk, and maintain the automobiles together. Working together allows great teaching moments. Families used to have to work together to survive, but in today's world, work often pulls the family apart. Create a tradition of working together and make it a priority.

Pancakes and Projects

Saturday mornings make pancakes for breakfast. Plan a project that you would like to work on as a family. Each Saturday carry out your project. If this becomes a habit, children will know that they need to get their project done before they play.

Ten-Minute Program

At the end of the day everyone takes ten minutes to clean up the house. Many hands make light work!

Pillowcase Fun

Make pillowcases for each holiday. This is a fun way to build anticipation for the upcoming holiday.

Neighborhood Car Wash

Put up signs or hand out flyers announcing that there will be a car wash at your house the following Saturday. Invite neighbors to come over and get their cars cleaned inside and out. Spend four hours cleaning cars together and provide this as a service to your neighbors!

Pizza Party

Make it known that on Friday nights at your house you will be making pizza. Invite friends over to play games and eat pizza. Continue this tradition for a month of Fridays and soon your friends will know that Friday night is pizza night at your house.

Sunday Visits

Sunday evenings are a great time for visiting family. Go see Grandma and Grandpa. If you don't have a grandma and grandpa that live nearby, adopt an elderly couple as your grandparents.

Family Reunions

Hold regularly scheduled family reunions for the extended family. Schedule this so everyone can plan their vacation around it.

Guess Who Paid

Take your family to a restaurant. Look around and choose a family. Instruct the waiter that you would like to anonymously pay for their meal. Leave without them knowing who paid and see how good you feel. (You could also do this at the gas pump.)

Connecting With Children
Families That Play Together, Stay Together

When all is said and done, the most valuable inheritance you will leave your child is the legacy of memories; of a home filled with love, timeless values, simple delights, homespun comforts, cherished traditions, joyous celebrations, and fond remembrance. These are treasures that can never be lost, stolen, or taken from you. They're the most important riches that will be your privilege to pass on.

This chapter gives you some parenting pointers and provides several ideas about how to connect with your children. Time passes too quickly, take time each day to let your kids know how much you love them.

WHAT KIDS NEED TO SUCCEED

A nationwide survey of 273,000 children grades six through twelve found thirty assets that kids need to succeed.

1. *Family support.* Hug them, verbally tell them how you feel, and spend time with them.
2. *Parent as a social resource.* Ask questions and listen to what they say.
3. *Parent communication.* Be available whenever, wherever, whatever.
4. *Other adult resources.* Expose your children to other adults who are positive.
5. *Other adult communication.* Include kids in conversations with other adults.
6. *Parent involvement at school.* Make it a point to know the teachers at your child's school.

7. *Positive school environment.* Ask about school, volunteer at their school.

8. *Parental standards.* Stand together on issues and discuss standards.

9. *Parental discipline.* Set rules with fair and reasonable consequences

10. *Parental monitoring.* Find out who your children will be with, what they will be doing, where they will be, and when they will be home.

11. *Time at home.* Make a goal to have them home four nights a week. Invite friends over on their at-home nights.

12. *Positive peer influence.* Get to know their friends and their friends' parents.

13. *Music.* Make music a part of everyday life in your home. If interested, have them take music lessons.

14. *Extracurricular activities.* Show support by attending events.

15. *Community activities.* Learn about events in your community and get children involved.

16. *Involvement in faith community.* Encourage active involvement in religious activities.

17. *Achievement motivation.* Be a role model for lifelong learning.

18. *Educational aspiration.* Discuss life goals and be a role model.

19. *School performance.* Affirm school success through family celebrations.

20. *Homework.* Provide a quiet environment conducive to studying.

21. *Helping people.* Seek opportunities to serve.

22. *Global concern.* Discuss world disasters and give to charity.

23. *Empathy.* Do not tolerate any put-downs or name calling in your home.

24. *Sexual Restraint.* Talk openly about sex, share your values, and make expectations clear.

25. *Assertiveness skills.* Be positive and affirming. Teach your children to stick up for what they believe in.

26. *Decision making skills.* Include your kids in decision making.

27. *Friendship skills.* Invite friends to your home and watch them interact.

28. *Planning skills.* Give your children responsibility. Set goals and prioritize.

29. *Self-esteem.* Express your love regularly and treat children with respect.

30. *Hope.* Inspire hope by being hopeful, looking forward to your future, and enjoying life.

(Peter L. Benson, PhD; Judy Galbraith; Pamela Espeland; *What Kids Need to Succeed: Proven, Practical Ways to Raise Good Kids* [Minneapolis: Free Spirit, 1998], 3-4.)

FOUR T'S OF CONNECTING WITH CHILDREN

1. *Time.* Spend quality time with each child.
2. *Talk.* Ask questions, initiate conversations, and show interest in what they are interested in.
3. *Touch.* Pat them on the back, give hugs, and connect with them physically.
4. *Tradition.* Develop traditions that they can count on.

(Studio 5, KSL Television and Radio, Salt Lake City, a division of Bonneville International, Dr. Liz Hale segment, *Connecting with Children*.)

THE EIGHT FORMULA: TEACH, TEST, TRUST

- The first eight years you teach your children.
- The second eight years you test what you taught.
- The third eight years you trust them.

TEN POSITIVES TO ONE NEGATIVE

If you say or do one negative thing to your children, it takes ten positive things to erase the negative.

THREE SIMPLE WAYS TO CONNECT

1. Make time for each other.
2. Improve communication.
3. Emphasize values.

MAKE EVERY MINUTE COUNT

Take time out from what you are doing when your children come home. Look at them, sit by them, ask them about their day, and look through their backpack. Show genuine interest in them.

JUST YOU AND ME, KID

Have a special night for just you and each of your children. You don't need to do something expensive or complicated. Let the child choose what you are going to do. Some ideas for outings:

what you are going to do. Some ideas for outings:

- Go for a walk or a bike ride.
- Read a book together or go to the library.
- Make a treat together.
- Go out and get ice cream.
- Play a game together.
- Go outside and kick or throw a ball to each other.

When you take your child on the one-on-one outings, let him lead the conversation. Don't correct or lecture your child. Let him talk. Let him make the agenda. If he chooses something that you aren't particularly fond of remember you are there to be supportive. Go with his plan!

DOOR DECORATING

When a child accomplishes something great, decorate his bedroom door. Each person in the family could write a little note and tape it to the door. Write nice things on heart-shaped paper and tape it to the door. Make a candy bar note and attach it to the door.

GET INVOLVED WITH YOUR CHILDREN'S ACTIVITIES

- Attend their sporting events. Be their biggest fan.
- Volunteer at their school.
- Invite friends over, get to know them, and watch your children interact with them.
- Help with homework, and show genuine interest in what they are learning.
- Encourage them to develop new talents and point out positive characteristics that they have.

TURN OFF THE TELEVISION

You can't concentrate on each other if your eyes and ears are locked to the television. Instead, make a craft, read a book together, play in the sandbox or in the snow, go to a park to play, make a kite and go fly it, or play a board game.

MAKE CHORES FUN

- Write a list of chores that need to be done. Cut them into strips and put them in a bowl. Each person draws their chores out of the bowl.

- Write down chores and time limits for the chores on paper. Cut them in small strips and put them into a bottle. Sit in a circle and spin the bottle. When the bottle stops, the person who it is pointing to opens it up and chooses a slip of paper. They must complete the chore in the amount of time given.
- Go shopping. Give everyone a basket and tell them they get to go shopping for items. Look around the house and pick up anything that is out of place and put the items back where they belong.

COUPON BOOKS

Stash a coupon in their backpack. Make it good for something such as a night out, playing a game of their choice, a pedicure party, a favorite treat, one day free from chores, or a movie night.

LUNCHBOX NOTES

Tuck a note into their lunchbox before school. The notes should let them know that you think they are great. Some ideas for things to say or do in the notes:

- Good luck on your test. Remember, be like frozen orange juice and concentrate!
- Make a picture note. Draw an eye (I), heart (love), ewe (you)!
- Give them a coupon that they can redeem when they get home. Make the coupon multiple choice; let them choose which item they want such as a favorite treat, a night off chores, or a pillow fight.
- I believe in you.
- I'm there for you.
- Just because I think you're great.
- You're very dependable and I'm proud of you.
- Remember your appointment today.
- I love you just the way you are.

SECRET SERVICE FAMILY

Draw names for the week. Do a secret act of service for that child each day of the week. At the end of the week the child gets to guess if Mom or Dad was their secret pal. You could do this with the whole family and have each person draw a name for the week.

JOURNALING

Purchase notebooks or journals for each member of your family. Each week write a journal entry on one of the following subjects:

- Tell the story of your birth.
- Tell about a favorite memory from when you were a toddler.
- Tell about your favorite birthday.
- Write about your favorite holiday.
- Tell about a camping trip.
- Tell what your favorite vacation has been.
- Write about your friends.
- Tell about school; write about the subjects you like and don't like, teachers, and lunch.
- Tell about your family using three words to describe each family member.
- List some of your talents.

BIRTHDAY PARTIES

Let each child know he is special on his birthday. Plan parties that he will remember forever. Following are some party pointers for kids birthday parties.

- *Dinosaur Party.* Make bone-shaped invitations, decorate with dinosaur footprints, and mark place settings with a rock with the child's name on it. Have a boulder bust: make piñatas with paper sacks, and fill with candy and toys. Use a bat as the club to break the piñata. Have an egg toss and dig for fossil treasures. Serve "dino-dogs" (hot dogs) and dinosaur jell-o eggs for snacks.
- *Princess Party.* Make invitations in the shape of a crown and instruct guests to dress as their favorite princess. Play pin the crown on the princess, or pin the kiss on the frog. Make necklaces and have purses filled with party favors for each guest to take home.
- *Construction Party.* Send toy dump truck invitations saying, "Birthday party under construction." Decorate the party with construction tape and let children play with blocks in the "Work Zone." Have a tool treasure hunt. Serve cake and ice cream out of a large toy dump truck.
- *Circus Party.* Send your guests tickets to a circus at your house. Give them four tickets: admission, refreshments, makeup, and

tightrope walk. Hire a clown to come and entertain. Send guests home with balloons, and a photo of them with the clown.

- *Space Party.* Make invitations in the shape of a rocket. Cover the table with aluminum foil and hang planets above the table. Make spaceships out of boxes, using various lids from containers as controls, and get ready for take off. Launch rockets by threading a straw with yarn, blowing up a balloon, and putting the balloon on the end of the straw. Let go. Serve space ice cream for dessert.

- *Wizard Party.* Make an invitation from a CD. On the CD, write, "Prediction: a magical time at . . . " then give the party information. Serve magic potions for a drink. Fill jars with various kinds of soda. Have a jelly bean tasting contest, or a treasure hunt. Write the clues backwards and give them a mirror to help decode the clues.

- *Farm Adventure.* Invite guests with an invitation tied around the neck of a small plastic farm animal. Set up the party outside. Search for prizes in a stack of straw, and play animal charades.

- *Sports Day.* Write the party information on a ball and deliver to each guest. Play a game of kickball. Make a ball toss, and give them prizes if they make it through the hole. Fill sports bottles with a variety of party favors for the guests to take home. Serve refreshments that would normally be served at a ball game.

- *Pirate Party.* Photocopy a map of your neighborhood. Circle your house and print all the party information on the back. Make treasure boxes and go on a treasure hunt. Play pirate games: divide the group into two and have each crew make a ship out of a box. Then, throw ping-pong balls back and forth at each ship. Serve sailboat pizzas and treasure chest cake.

- *Wild West Cowboy Party.* Make wanted-poster invitations. Decorate the party like a covered wagon. Go panning for gold (sprinkle coins in a box of sand) and have a stick horse relay. Place party favors inside a red bandana for everyone to take home.

- *Fishing Expedition.* Use a die cut of a fish with the party information on it for the invitations. Make a fish pond out of a large box and let the children fish for prizes. Play fish concentration. Send home a tackle box made from an egg carton and fill the egg holes with fish crackers, gummy fish, string licorice (fishing line), and gum balls (bobbers).

- *Luau Party.* Decorate the party as if you were in Hawaii. Send surfboard invitations. Greet each guest with a Hawaiian lei. Do the limbo and set up a photo backdrop and take pictures. Make mango ice cream or fruit smoothies for a treat.
- *Candyland Party.* Set up your house like the candyland game (chocolate swamp, gumdrop mountain, lollypop land, candy castle, and so forth). Play a game at each spot. Make candy necklaces, have a treasure hunt, and do a candy basket scramble.
- *Color-Coded Party.* Use a color and make the invitations, games, treats, and favors all out of that color.
- *Other.* Other party theme ideas are a pop star party, pizza party, olympics party, train party, fun in the sun party, Chinatown party, all-American baseball party, and detective party.

CANDY BAR NOTES

A simple and fun way to let your child know you are thinking of him is to write a candy bar message. Leave the candy bar note in his "mailbox," on his pillow, or stuff it in his backpack. You could even take it to his school and have it delivered. Some candy bar messages include:

- *Mounds.* You're mounds of fun.
- *Sweet Tarts.* Thanks for being a sweetheart.
- *Snickers.* I love your snickers and smiles.
- *Chocolate Kiss.* Here's a great big kiss from me.
- *M&M's.* You are *most marvelous.
- *Starburst.* To a super star!
- *Almond Joy.* It is a joy to be your Mom or Dad.
- *Nestlé Treasure.* I treasure you.

TREAT TALK

You can write a note on a simple treat to let them know you care.

- *Doughnuts* Do not forget how much I love you.
- *Strawberry* I love you berry much.
- *Hostess Snowball* You're some bunny special (attach paper rabbit ears).
- *Cookie* You are one smart cookie!

ART AND ACCOMPLISHMENTS GALLERY

Designate a wall in your home to show off your child's artwork, report cards, awards, and other accomplishments.

RAISE YOUR CHILD'S EQ

EQ stands for emotional quotient. It is the ability for you to deal with emotions. Children who are self-aware, who know how to read people, who are adaptable, flexible, and self confident are the ones who flourish in life. Rate your child's EQ by answering a few questions. Put a 1 by things that are rarely true, a 2 by things that are sometimes true, and a 3 by things that are often true.

- Does your child
  - › Easily talk about his emotions?
  - › Know various words to describe feelings?
  - › Have empathy and sympathy for others?
  - › Have an optimistic attitude?
  - › Wait patiently for something he wants?
  - › Have goals and an idea or a plan to reach goals?
  - › Know how to solve problems independently?
  - › Listen attentively?
  - › Know what he needs and how to ask for it?
  - › Handle himself well in a group of kids his own age?
- Do you
  - › Know what you're feeling most of the time?
  - › Try to understand someone else's point of view, even in an argument?
  - › Have an optimistic, hopeful outlook?
  - › Regularly share your feelings with others?
  - › Control your temper, even when stressed?
  - › Have goals and plans for achieving these goals?
  - › Know how to listen carefully and restate what has been said?
  - › Consider all options when making a decision?
  - › Know how to figure out your needs and fulfill them?
  - › Find time to laugh with loved ones?

Add up your child's points and your points separately.

- › 10–15 points: Focus on giving yourself and your child EQ time every day without fail.
- › 16–24 points: You are in okay shape, there is still room for improvement.
- › 25 or more points: You are an EQ star! Keep up the good work

(Henig, R.M. "Measuring Emotional Intelligence in Adolescents." *McCall's*, June 1996, 91.)

THREE IMPORTANT WORDS

Tell your kids that you love them every day. Tell them in words and actions. There is no better foundation for a child than to know that his parents love him and care enough to show him every day!

Self-esteem develops in your child through all the experiences in his lifetime. Be sure to spend time alone with each of your children and say the words that are most important to him: "I love you!" Hugs, gifts, and toys might be easier for you to use as signs of love, but the words are much more important.

LEARNING YOUR CHILD'S LOVE LANGUAGE

Think about each child.

- Does your child thrive on being told that they are doing something good? Does he like to hear I love you? His love language is *tell me.*
- Does your child like hugs and kisses? Does he like to sit by you and cuddle? His love language is *touch me.*
- Does your child like little gifts? Does he like it if you do something for them? His love language is *show me.*

There is an actual love language quiz you can take. John L. Lund has written a book, *The Five Languages of Love.* This love language quiz in his book.

Storybook Lessons That Teach Values

Paving the Path to Success Through Reading

Family activities can be happy experiences that foster unity. Building strong unified relationships within a family requires family members to spend time together. As they work, play, learn, and worship together, a family grows in the ability to influence each other and build lasting bonds.

One way to help family members learn values that contribute to the well-being of the family unit is through sharing stories that can influence character. This section of the book provides lesson ideas that teach a value with a story, a discussion topic, an activity, and a refreshment idea.

These lessons can be adapted to fit your family's needs. The stories suggested are only suggestions. There are many stories, fables, and favorite series of books you may use which are not listed.

Look over the lesson ideas. Choose one that you would like to try and get started. Have fun with your family as you learn and grow together.

Discussion Topic: Agency and Making Good Choices
Story: *Sam and the Firefly*, by Philip D. Eastman
Activity: Play flashlight tag
Refreshment: Use a cookie cutter to cut cheese in the shape of a butterfly. Decorate the cheese with olives to look like a firefly.

Discussion Topic: Having a Positive Attitude
Story: *The Little Engine That Could*, Platt and Munk All Aboard Book
Activity: Go on a train ride or do a challenging obstacle course where willpower and effort are needed in order to achieve success.

Refreshment: Make candy trains out of a small pack of gum for the car, red and white peppermints for the wheels, and a caramel and a candy kiss for the engine.

Discussion Topic: Believe in Yourself
Story: *Stand Tall Molly Lou Melon*, by Patty Lovell
Activity: Each person in the family gets a paper with his name written at the top. Pass the papers around and everyone writes good qualities about the person whose name is at the top. Continue until everyone has written on all papers.
Refreshment: 100 Grand candy bars

Discussion Topic: Bodies
Story: *Parts*, by Tedd Arnold
Activity: Five sense activity.
- Eyes: Play "I spy."
- Ears: Play "Name That Tune."
- Hands: Fill a brown bag with small items like cotton balls, feathers, or combs. Each person must reach into bag and guess what he is touching.
- Smell: Fill jars with different things to smell and have everyone guess what he is smelling.
- Taste: Jelly bean guess. Buy a bag of jelly belly jelly beans. Pass out the same flavor to every member of the family and have them guess what flavor they are tasting.

Refreshment: Jelly beans

Discussion Topic: Charity
Story: *The Giving Tree*, by Shel Silverstein
Activity: Give a helping hand to someone in your community who could use a lift.
Refreshment: Sliced apples with caramel dip

Discussion Topic: Compassion
Story: *Stone Soup*, by Jon Muth
Activity: Make a soup where each family member adds an ingredient.
Refreshment: Soup

Discussion Topic: Determination
Story: *The Princess Knight*, by Cornelia Funke
Activity: Run races in your backyard.
Refreshment: Gatorade, bananas, trail mix, and other race food

Discussion Topic: Differences
Story: *The Ugly Duckling*, by Hans Christian Andersen
Activity: Go swimming
Refreshment: Ducks made out of a half a twinkie for the body, two jelly candy orange slices for wings (use toothpicks to stick wings into body), an orange tic-tac for the beak, and two small chocolate chips for the eyes.

Discussion Topic: Example
Story: *One-of-a-Kind Mallie*, by Kimberly Brubaker Bradley
Activity: Have each person choose someone who has been a good example to them. Invite all the good examples to a dinner at your house.
Refreshment: Thank-you dinner for good examples

Discussion Topic: Fairness
Story: *Alexander and the Terrible, Horrible, No Good, Very Bad Day*, by Judith Viorst
Activity: Play a game like Sorry or Aggravation to teach good sportsmanship.
Refreshment: Pizza. Cut the pizza unevenly and serve large slices to some family members and small slices to others.

Discussion Topic: Family
Story: *Love Is a Family*, by Roma Downey
Activity: Take family pictures.
Refreshment: Heart-shaped sugar cookies

Discussion Topic: Forgiveness
Story: *Under the Lemon Moon*, by Edith Hope Fine
Activity: Pack a backpack full of rocks. Discuss how holding grudges and not forgiving is like carrying the backpack full of rocks. Go through the process of forgiving, and as you discuss each step remove rocks from the backpack. Sum it all up by stating that forgiving lightens our load.
Refreshment: Lemon bars, lemonade, or lemon meringue pie

Discussion Topic: Friends
Story: *Rainbow Fish*, by Marcus Pfister
Activity: Invite friends over to a party at your house.
Refreshment: Goldfish crackers, or fish candies

Discussion Topic: Golden Rule
Story: *The Ant and the Elephant*, by Bill Peet
Activity: Split the family in two. Each group does nice things for the other. Set a time limit to see who can do the most nice things in the set time frame.
Refreshment: Make ants by taking a pretzel rod and using icing to attach three whopper malted milk balls on the end of the pretzel rod.

Discussion Topic: Gratitude
Story: *Saying Thank You*, by Colleen L. Reece
Activity: Have a wipeout-ingratitude relay race. Purchase two containers of wipes and place each container on a chair at one end of a room. Divide the family into two teams. On cue, each team runs to a wipe container and gets one wipe and runs back to the next person, that person then goes and gets a wipe. The team whose wipe container is empty first, wins.
You could also have each family member write a thank-you note to someone who has been helpful to him. Make cookies and deliver them with the notes.
Refreshment: Caramel Popcorn (use the wipes to clean up sticky hands)

Discussion Topic: Happiness
Story: *Dragon of the Red Dawn*, by Mary Pope Osborne
Activity: Play the smile game. One person is "it" and goes to the center of the circle. He tries to get anyone in the family to smile or laugh by doing and saying crazy things. The first person to smile is "it" next.
Refreshment: Cupcakes

Discussion Topic: Helping Others
Story: *Good Job, Little Bear*, by Martin Waddell
Activity: Mow someone's lawn, shovel snow, or rake leaves.
Refreshment: Chocolate chip cookies (for "chipping" in)

Discussion Topic: Home
Story: *All the Places to Love*, by Patricia MacLachlan
Activity: Guessing game. Have each family member guess each other's favorite place around your home.
Refreshment: Homemade bread and jam

Discussion Topic: Honesty
Story: *The Big Fat Enormous Lie*, by Marjorie Weinman Sharmat
Story: *The Empty Pot*, by Demi
Activity: Get two pieces of rope. One rope has several knots tied in it and the other is plain. Show how the knotted rope is shorter than the other rope. Compare the ropes. Which one would be easiest to play jump rope, with? Tow a car? Compare the rope to our lives. Sometimes our lives get knotted up with lies. When we get that way we are not very useful. Lies are like knots in a rope—nothing but trouble.
Refreshment: Licorice ropes

Discussion Topic: Integrity
Story: *Mufaro's Beautiful Daughters*, by John Steptoe
Activity: Discuss how you reap what you sow. In your journal, write characteristics that you would like to develop in yourself.
Refreshment: Sunflower seeds.

Discussion Topic: Judging Others
Story: *Hunchback of Notre Dame*, retold by Gina Ingoglia
Activity: Get two eggs. Make a small hole in each end of one of the eggs and blow the inside out. Make the other egg dirty and unappealing on the outside. Hold up the two eggs and ask which egg they would like to eat. Hold up the clean one and crush it in your hand. Crack the dirty egg and show how clean and good it is inside. Discuss how you look at peers, strangers, and neighbors. We cannot judge others merely by their appearance, or first impression.
Refreshment: Omelets

Discussion Topic: Kindness
Story: *Sassafras*, by Stephen Cosgrove
Activity: "Catch kindness week." Draw names in your family and do secret acts of kindness for that person all week. At next week's lesson, reveal who

you were doing kind things for. Discuss how being kind increases feelings of love in your family.
Refreshment: Ice cream cones

Discussion Topic: Labels
Story: *You are Special*, by Max Lucado
Activity: Star gazing. Go outside and look at the stars, find the constellations, wish upon shooting stars, and enjoy being together as a family.
Refreshment: Starbursts

Discussion Topic: Listening
Story: *Come Along, Daisy!* by Jane Simmons
Activity: Go on a scavenger hunt together. Look for some of the things Daisy saw. Stay together as a family and discuss the importance of listening to and obeying parents.
Refreshment: Rice crispy treats. Listen to them go snap, crackle, and pop.

Discussion Topic: Love
Story: *Guess How Much I Love You*, by Sam McBratney
Activity: Each person thinks of creative ways to show or tell how much they love a family member. Concentrate on showing your love for family this week.
Refreshment: Make smoothies and discuss how showing love makes family life "smoother."

Discussion Topic: Loyalty to Family and Friends
Story: *Paperboy*, by Mary Kay Kroeger
Activity: Write down names of people who are loyal to your family. Think of people who you should be loyal to. Each person writes down one way that they will show loyalty. Make newspaper boats and put your idea in your boat and let it float down a stream.
Refreshment: Root beer floats

Discussion Topic: Manners
Story: *Fancy Nancy*, by Jane O'Connor
Activity: Serve an etiquette dinner. Teach table manners, phone manners, and social manners.
Refreshment: Etiquette dinner

Discussion Topic: Names
Story: *Chrysanthemum*, by Kevin Henkes
Activity: Play the name game. Discuss how each person got their name and what it means. Write out your name and by each letter of your name write an adjective to describe you. Display your name posters for the week.
Refreshment: Alphabet cereal

Discussion Topic: Neighbors
Story: *Mercy Watson to the Rescue*, by Kate DiCamillo
Activity: Play freeze tag. If the person who is "it" tags someone, they must freeze. Players who have not been tagged can release frozen players. The last person to get frozen is "it" for the next round.
Refreshment: Popsicles

Discussion Topic: Obedience
Story: *Pokey Little Puppy*, by Janette Sebring Lowery
Activity: Play "Mother May I" or "Simon Says."
Refreshment: Strawberry shortcake

Discussion Topic: Participation, Do Your Share
Story: *The Little Red Hen*, by Paul Galdone
Activity: Make wheat bread together. Grind the wheat, mix the dough, shape the loaves, and bake the bread.
Refreshment: Wheat bread

Discussion Topic: Patience
Story: *Wemberly's Ice-Cream Star*, by Kevin Henkes
Activity: Put a large puzzle together as a family. Discuss patience as you find where the puzzle pieces should go.
Refreshment: Ice cream

Discussion Topic: Peer Pressure
Story: *The Emperor's New Clothes*, by Hans Christian Andersen
Activity: Look through magazines and cut out advertisements that are trying to persuade you to do things. Talk about peer pressure and how to avoid falling into peer pressure.
Refreshment: Go to a store and allow each family member to choose a treat. Have everyone tell why they chose the treat they did.

Discussion Topic: Problem Solving
Story: *Alicia's Best Friends*, by Lisa Jahn-Clough
Activity: Give each person in your family two dollars and explain that they are going to throw a party but they only have two dollars. Go to the store and let them shop for treats, games, and other party supplies. Let them work together to solve the budget problem.
Refreshment: Party treats

Discussion Topic: Quarreling
Story: *Let's Be Friends Again*, by Hans Wilhelm
Activity: We can disagree without becoming disagreeable. Role-play different situations when you could either fight or work the problem out together.
Refreshment: Serve something that can be broken in half and shared: cookies, soft pretzels, candy bars, and so forth.

Discussion Topic: Respect for Community
Story: *Wartville Wizard*, by Don Madden
Activity: Clean up your neighborhood.
Refreshment: Doughnuts: "donut" leave garbage in your community.

Discussion Topic: Respect for the Elderly
Story: *Grampa-Lop*, by Stephen Cosgrove
Activity: Visit grandparents or a retirement home. Ask questions about their lives and learn about them.
Refreshment: Serve pie, and bring enough to share with those you visit.

Discussion Topic: Respect for Parents
Story: *Everyone Else's Parents Said Yes*, by Paula Danziger
Activity: Play "Spin the Bottle" with the theme of "Honoring Your Parents." On small slips of paper write things that you as parents expect from your children. Play spin the bottle. When the bottle points to a person, that person gets to draw out a slip of paper and tell how they can show honor to their parents by doing what the paper says.
Refreshment: Tootsie Pops

Discussion Topic: Respect for Self
Story: *The Luckiest One of All*, by Bill Peet

Activity: Self-portraits. Make a collage of things about yourself. Show the collages one at a time and have the other family members guess whose collage it is.
Refreshment: Popcorn balls

Discussion Topic: Responsibility
Story: *Blueberries for Sal*, by Robert McCloskey
Activity: Go to a berry patch and pick berries. Play the game twenty questions while picking berries. The topics should all be about responsibility and you can only ask yes or no questions.
Refreshment: Make something with the berries you picked.

Discussion Topic: Rules
Story: *No Laughing, No Smiling, No Giggling*, by James Stevenson
Activity: Play "Add-on Follow the Leader. The leader does an action such as dribbling or shooting a ball, or throwing it up in the air. The leader then passes the ball on and the next family member does that action and adds their own action on the end. Continue until someone forgets what action comes next.
Refreshment: Make saltwater taffy. Make sure you follow the rules of the recipe exactly and show how following rules makes life sweeter.

Discussion Topic: Sacrifice
Story: *The Legend of the Bluebonnet*, retold by Tomie de Paola
Activity: Each person chooses one of their favorite things and gives it to another person in the family or someone who they know would love it. Show how sacrificing makes us appreciate our blessing more.
Refreshment: Cinnamon rolls

Discussion Topic: Self-Control
Story: *When I Feel Angry*, by Cornelia Spelman
Activity: Introduce the idea of counting to ten before speaking or acting out when upset. Ask your family why counting to ten would help in a volatile situation. Ask for other ideas for controlling your temper. Encourage family members to work on self-control this week.
Refreshment: Pop Rocks: don't explode when you get angry.

Discussion Topic: Service
Story: *Johnny Appleseed* (John Chapman Biography), by Steven Kellogg
Activity: Do a service project for someone you know.
Refreshment: Apple crisp or apple pie

Discussion Topic: Talents
Story: *Batter Up Wombat*, by Helen Lester
Activity: Spotlight each member of your family. Show off their talents. Make sure each family member feels loved and special.
Refreshment: Have someone in your family who is talented at cooking or baking make their favorite treat to share.

Discussion Topic: Trust
Story: *The Boy Who Cried Wolf*, by Carol Barnett
Activity: Play the definition game. Look up words in the dictionary and have each family member make up a definition for that word. One person reads all the definitions and the correct definition from the dictionary. The family members try to guess what the correct definition is.
Refreshment: Muffins

Discussion Topic: Unconditional Love
Story: *Love You Forever*, by Robert Munsch
Activity: Sit in a circle and hold hands. Show how a circle has no end, and explain that your love for your family will go on forever. While sitting in the circle, play "Do You Love Your Neighbor?" One person is "it" and asks another family member if they love their neighbor. That family member says, "Yes but I don't love people who . . ." ending with a statement that will make others in the circle move. The people in the circle who fit the description have to get up and quickly change chairs. The person in the center tries to steal one of the empty chairs. The person left without a chair is "it" for the next round.
Refreshment: Pigs in a blanket (hot dogs wrapped in bread dough) Explain that your love will always wrap around your family.

Discussion Topic: Understanding
Story: *A Special Raccoon*, by Kim Carlisle
Activity: Help your family think of others who might be struggling with something. Encourage them to think of what they must be feeling and

then think of something to do for those people. Play a new game as a family. Help each family member understand how to play.
Refreshment: Brownies

Discussion Topic: Unity
Story: *Bundle of Sticks*, Aesops fable
Activity: Give each person in your family a popsicle stick and see if they can break the stick in half. Put a bundle of sticks together and see if they can break the bundle in half. Explain that by staying unified as a family, everyone is stronger.
Refreshment: String licorice: pull off a string of licorice and think of a way that your family can become more unified.

Discussion Topic: Unselfishness
Story: *Zamani Goes to Market*, by Muriel L. Feelings
Activity: Set up a tray of desserts that are different. Make sure you put something on the tray that is least likely to be chosen. Choose a family member to go around the room and let each family member choose a dessert. Emphasize that he is letting others choose first. Discuss the importance of unselfish behavior.
Refreshment: Eat the desserts that are on the tray.

Discussion Topic: Work
Story: *Mister Penny*, by Marie Hall Ets
Activity: Penny pitch work session. Have each family member pitch two pennies. If both pennies land with heads up, that family member goes to a jar that has slips of paper with jobs written on them. That person must draw a slip of paper and go complete the task in two minutes. The other family members keep pitching pennies. The game is over when all the jobs in the jar are finished.
Refreshment: Go to a store that sells penny candy. Let each person choose some penny candy.

Growing Together With Games

Children Need Your Presence More Than Your Presents

Spending quality time with your family is an important tool in building family unity. Instead of turning on the television, or driving around without interacting, play games. Games are a great way to get to know each other better. You can see how each member of your family reacts to winning or losing.

Take advantage of times when you are waiting for an appointment, traveling in a car, or sitting at home. Play games with your children. It will make them feel important and it will improve your relationship with them.

This chapter provides several games. Some of the games can be played in a few minutes with no preparation, while some require you to plan ahead. Either way, this chapter is all about fun! These game ideas have been collected from ideas given to me by others.

GUESSING GAMES

What Am I?

Write down different names or objects that go with your party theme. Tape a different name to each person's back without letting him read it. Have everyone try to figure out who they are by asking others yes-or-no questions. The first person to correctly guess who they are wins.

Body Part Game

Before the party take close-up pictures of different body parts such as eye, ear, elbow, knee, toes, fingers, and nose. Pass the pictures around and see if anyone can guess which body part it is and who it belongs to.

Song Charades

One at a time, each music fan uses only actions to depict a popular song title. Whoever guesses the song correctly gets to act out the next title.

Two-Person Charades

Split the whole group up into two teams. Each team will be given a bowl full of concepts they must act out. Two people from each team will choose a concept from the bowl that they must act out together. The objective of the game is to try and get your team to guess as many concepts as possible and beat the other team. As party planners you may use props or other ideas that will make the game more interesting.

Sticktionary

Let each group have a pile of toothpicks. This is the same game as pictionary but they use toothpicks, placed end to end, to "draw" their picture.

Two Truths and a Lie

Everyone sits in a circle. One person starts by getting the person next to him to tell two truths and one lie about his day. The first person has to guess which one is the lie. If he is right they get to sit down. If he guesses wrong, he goes on to the next person until he can guess correctly.

Hangman

Play hangman with different categories such as names, places, fruits, vegetables, sports, and cars. Break into two groups. Have one team guess the word; if they get the word before they are hung, they get a point.

Don't Eat Pete

Draw silly faces on each square of a bingo grid. Place small candies over all the faces. Have one person leave the room. All other players choose one face to be Pete. The player who is it, comes back and starts to pick up the candies off the faces one by one, as soon as that player picks up the candy covering Pete, everyone yells, "Don't eat Pete!" That player's turn is finished at that point.

The Book Game

Lay out nine books on the floor in rows of three. One of you who knows the trick is the pointer. Have one person go out of the room and the group chooses one of the books. The person then comes back and guesses which book the group chose as the pointer points to them.

As you point, touch the part of the chosen book that is the same as its place among the nine books. For example, if the chosen book is the top middle book, point in the top and middle of that book when pointing to it. Keep playing until everyone has had the chance to guess, and figures out the trick to the game.

Word Play Dictionary Game

Each person writes down unfamiliar words. Players take turns announcing their chosen word to the group and definers write what they think the word means on a slip of paper. Players then read their guesses out loud; the chooser of the word reveals its true definition. Award one point to anyone who guessed correctly. If nobody guesses right, award a point to the chooser of the word.

Hot and Cold

One person stays in the room to hide an object while everyone else steps out. When the object is hidden, he invites the others back into the room and has them search for the object. The hider gets to say if they are getting hot (close to the object) or cold (far from the object). The first person who finds the object gets to hide it in the next round.

Sound Charades

Write down several noisemaking items (household appliances work well) on small pieces of paper and put the slips in a bowl. Select one person to go first. He will draw a slip of paper and make sounds associated with that item. The other players try to guess what the item is. This game can also be played with animal noises.

Mystery Bag

Fill a brown paper bag full of various items. One person reaches in the bag and feels what is in there for one minute. When finished, that person writes down what he thinks is in the bag. When everyone has had a chance to feel the items and write their guesses, reveal what is in the bag. The person with the most correct guesses wins.

Who's the Leader?

Choose one child as the guesser and send him out of the room. Pick another child to be the leader; everyone else is a follower. The leader's job is to direct the followers (without saying a word) with actions such as winking, whistling, or snapping fingers. Each action should last about ten seconds. Whenever he makes a change, the followers must instantly mimic him. Once the leader has begun, call the guesser back into the room and see how long it takes him to figure out who the leader is.

Famous People

Fill a bowl with names of famous people. You will need to come up with 100–200 names. The person who is it reaches in the bowl and without saying names tries to describe the person whose name they drew out. Each person gets one minute to describe as many names as he can.

Out of Place

Find out who's most observant in your house. Ask everyone to leave the room. Now move seven items out of place and then invite everyone to come back in. The first person to spot everything that is wrong gets the next turn.

PARTY GAMES

Flour Castles

Build castles out of flour. Give each team some cups, buckets, spoons, and other building materials. Allow them ten minutes to construct their castle. When time is up, judge the flour castles.

Puzzle Pairing

Hand out puzzle pieces. Use as many puzzles as you choose to divide the group. Participants must then mingle to find out which puzzle they belong to. As the participants assemble and put together their puzzle, they will figure out which team they are on. The group to put their puzzle together first wins.

Marble Roulette

You will need one dozen marbles, all the same size. Wet a paper towel and gently squeeze it. Stretch it taut over a glass and fasten it with a rubber band. To play, kids take turns placing a marble on the towel; whoever adds the marble that breaks through the towel loses.

Candy Bar Game

Buy twenty assorted candy bars. Put the candy bars in a pile in the middle of the circle and put a pair of dice in a pie plate. Pass the dice around. If you roll a double, a seven, or an eleven, choose a candy bar from the pile. Or, you can steal a candy bar from someone else if they have one you want. Set the timer for ten minutes. You have to keep the candy bar you have in your hands. If you want the game to move faster, use two pie plates and have the dice going two different directions.

Flour Shave Off

Firmly pack a cup of flour (the longer and narrower the cup is, the more difficult the game will be). Turn the cup upside down on a plate and carefully pull the cup off the flour. Place a penny on top of the flour. One by one, players use a butter knife to shave away portions of the flour. The one who makes the flour tower fall has to get the penny out using their mouth and no hands.

Man And Snake

Give each player three large craft sticks. Make the game pieces with sticks. Draw a snake on one side of two of the sticks and a person on one side of the third. To play, each person tosses all three of his sticks in the air at the same time, keeping their sticks separate from everyone else's. Record how they land and tally each player's score. The first person to score twenty points wins the round.

- Scoring chart:
  › 1 blank, 1 snake, 1 man=0 points,
  › 3 blanks=1 point
  › 2 snakes, 1 man=1 point
  › 2 snakes, 1 blank=2 points
  › 2 blanks, 1 snake=2 points
  › 2 blanks, 1 man=3 points

Cracker Whistler

Give two crackers to each participant. When the signal is given, they are to eat the crackers. The first one who can whistle is the winner.

Cooks Corner

Blindfold one person; give that person a large bowl full of miniature marshmallows and a wooden spoon. Set a kitchen timer for one minute and let that person scoop as many marshmallows into another bowl as he can. Count the marshmallows after each person's turn.

This game can also be played with cotton balls; or by filling a bowl with rice and a box of small safety pins, and trying to dig the safety pins out of the rice.

Ping-Pong Puff

Establish two goal lines at opposite ends of a rug. Place a ping-pong ball in the center of the rug and hand each player a drinking straw. On cue, both players try to blow the ball past the opponent's goal line.

Straight Face Endurance

You will need one comic and several glum-faced challengers. The comic's mission is to make funny faces, tell jokes, or make funny noises to bring on a laugh. The first one in the crowd to crack a smile is the next comic.

M&M Game

Give each person ten M&M's of all different colors. Sit in a circle. One person takes an M&M out of his stash with his eyes closed. Depending on what color is picked he will have to tell something about himself. You can use these suggestions or come up with your own.

- *Red* Share something scary that has happened to you.
- *Blue* Share something nobody else knows about you.
- *Green* Share a dream you have.
- *Orange* Share something you like about yourself.
- *Brown* Share something you are afraid of.
- *Yellow* Share an embarrassing moment.

Pass The Parcel

Wrap a present. Rather than just having one present inside, wrap the present many times and insert small surprises between each wrapping. Play music as the parcel is passed around. When the music stops, the person holding the parcel gets to open one layer and see what surprise he gets. Continue until everyone has had a chance to unwrap.

Blowing Out The Candle

One player is blindfolded. He is moved back three steps, turned around, and permitted to take three steps before blowing. The object is to blow out the candle resting on a table. If you think it's easy, try it!

Penny Pitch

Set a tablecloth on a table. Tape different colored paper circles on the tablecloth. Give each person ten pennies. They get to pitch pennies from a designated starting line. If the penny lands in a circle, they get a prize.

Human Scavenger Hunt

Everyone is given a list of things to find among others in the group. The person who meets the criteria signs on the line following the statement. Some criteria you might use are:

1. Find someone who has the same birth month as you.

2. Find someone who ate cold cereal for breakfast.

Come up with a list of criteria such as these and see who can complete their list first!

Human Battleship

Divide the group into two teams. Put up a blanket so the teams can't see each other and have the kids position themselves like boats. Each team gets five chances to throw a missile (tennis ball or other soft ball). The object is to throw the ball over the blanket and hit the players on the other side to sink the other team's boats.

Bunco

The object of the game is to be the first player to score twenty-one points in a round. Each player takes a turn rolling three dice. One point is awarded for each six that is rolled. If a player rolls at least one six, he keeps rolling. If a player rolls three ones at once, he gets a wipeout and loses all the points he has received so far in that round. If a player rolls three sixes at once, that is a Bunco. As soon as a Bunco is rolled, all players try to grab the dice and score one point for each die snagged. Prizes are given for most rounds won, most rounds lost, and most buncos and wipeouts scored.

Ring Around the Chopsticks

Hide an odd number of colored rubber bands in a mound of sand. Give each player a chopstick. On cue, players kneel by the pile and plunge their sticks into the sand to skewer the rubber bands. When all the rubber bands have been uncovered, the player with the most on his stick wins.

Pulling Strings

Gather several balls of different colored string. Tie one end of the string to a party favor and hide it. Working backward, unravel the string through various obstacles and tie the free end to a stick. Repeat with all the colors of string. Give each participant a stick with string and have them follow it to his prize.

TREASURE HUNT IDEAS
- Draw a map for the group to follow.
- Think of clues to direct everyone to other clues, which lead to a buried treasure.
- Hand the group an item to put away, when they put it away they find something else out of place. Continue putting items away

until they find a treasure.
- Go letterboxing, or geo-caching.
- Draw pictures for clues.
- Make a color treasure hunt. Look for a certain color, or spray paint rocks different colors. Give each color a different point value and send them on the hunt, giving them a time limit. When everyone is back, add up the points to see who won.

GAME SHOW SPIN-OFFS

Play a family version of several game shows. Here are some shows that make great entertainment:
- Let's Make a Deal
- Who Wants to Be a Millionaire
- Newlywed Game
- Family Feud
- Wheel of Fortune
- Jeopardy
- Fear Factor
- Amazing Race
- Whose Line Is It Anyway
- Deal or No Deal
- American Idol
- Name That Tune
- Survivor

Evolution

Have everyone pretend to be an egg. Each person must find another egg to play "rock, paper, scissors" with. The winner evolves into a chicken, and the loser remains an egg. The chickens must find another chicken to play "rock, paper, scissors" with, while the eggs find other eggs to play with. The winners of the chickens evolve into a dinosaur, while the losers devolve back into an egg. They must continue playing "rock, paper, scissors" with others of their kind. The winners between the dinosaurs evolve into the highest form of evolution: Elvis.

ACTIVE GAMES

Dance Craze

Everyone writes a word on a slip of paper. Collect all the slips in a bowl. Take turns picking slips and making up dances to match the words.

Indoor Foot Volleyball

Tie a piece of yarn about one foot off the floor across a ten-foot area. Have everyone take off their shoes. Divide into two teams and have them set up crab style on each side of the string. Launch a ten-inch balloon into the air. The teams must kick the ball back and forth with their feet. If one team lets the balloon touch the floor, the other team earns a point and restarts the game by serving the balloon from their side. The first team to score fifteen points wins.

Indoor Hopscotch

Turn carpet samples into hopscotch squares by stenciling numbers on the samples. You will need three large carpet squares for the numbers two and three, five and six, and eight and nine. Use four small carpet squares for the numbers one, four, seven, and ten. Duct tape the carpet squares to your floor and play hopscotch any time of year.

Kick It

Tie twenty rubber bands together with another rubber band, like a hacky sack. See how many times you can kick it into the air before it hits the ground.

Thumping

Fill nylons with a half cup of flour and tie in knots. Gather outside in dark clothes. Give each person some ammunition (flour-filled nylons) and have a flour snowball fight. When you go back in the house see how many times each person was hit.

Flashlight Tag

This game is similar to regular tag, except you play in the dark, and tag by aiming your flashlight beam rather than tagging with your hands.

Flip Golf

You will need a quarter, small plastic containers, and a table. Set up a golf course on your table with plastic containers and a tee off box. Tee off by trying to flip the quarter into the plastic containers. Continue flipping the quarters from where they land. The player with the fewest flips is the winner.

Ping-Pong Basketball

Line two quart sized plastic containers with a paper towel. Dribble and shoot a ping-pong ball and try to score by bouncing the ball into the opposing player's basket. A basket after three dribbles is one point, after two dribbles is two points, and after one dribble is three points.

Ping-Pong Muffin Toss

Label the bottom of the muffin cups with point values. Try to gain the most points by making the ping-pong balls land in the muffin cups.

Hop Along Tag

The object of this game is to avoid being captured by the toad. Players can only move about by hopping on both feet. Define boundary lines in which the toad and the other players must remain throughout the game. Start hopping! If the toad tags another player that player must link arms with the toad's previous victim. The last untagged player wins the game.

Bowling Pin Derby

Set up ten plastic cup bowling pins in a triangular formation. Each player gets three consecutive rolls of a ball to knock down as many pins as possible. If all the pins fall before the third roll, reset them and continue. You get one point for each fallen pin.

Tabletop Hockey

Cut a plastic berry box in half. Invert one half and set it at one end of the table. Now your kids can line up at the opposite end and try to score by flicking buttons into the net.

Balloon Volley

Bat a balloon back and forth while linking arms with a partner, leaving one arm free to bat the balloon. Whichever pair is able to volley the balloon the longest wins.

A variation of this game is to volley the balloon while racing to the finish line. If the balloon touches the ground that team must start over.

Balloon Stomp

Each participant is given a string and a balloon, and instructed to blow up the balloon and tie it to his or her ankle. On the signal, everyone is instructed to try to stomp on each other's balloon. The last person that has an unpopped balloon tied to his ankle is the winner.

A variation of this game is to divide the group into two teams and give each team a certain color of balloon. They must try to stomp the balloons of the other team. The team with the most balloons left at the end wins.

Bubble Contest

Make bubble wands with a paper clip bent into a wand, a fly swatter, a hanger bent into a circle, or a hula hoop. Make bubbles by mixing one cup water, one-third cup dishwashing liquid, and two tablespoons light corn syrup or glycerin. Go to www.bubblemania.com for more bubble information.

Feather Vault

On cue, players try to blow their feathers overhead. Whoever keeps his feather aloft the longest without using hands is the winner.

Fancy Foot Race

Contestants must race to the finish line by placing one foot in front of the other, heel to toe, the entire length of the race way.

Obstacle Course Ideas

Set up an obstacle course using things around your house. You could use water balloons, a kiddie pool, golf balls, tires, and dress-up clothes. You may want to have players walk the plank, do a box hop, have a frisbee toss, or do a summer shower where players must balance a golf ball on a tee while walking through a sprinkler. You could also do a lawn chair slalom, or rake a ball a certain distance.

Egg Scramble

Select one person to start off as the bunny. The remaining players are the eggs, who quietly (so the bunny doesn't hear) select a color for themselves. Next, decide on a home base for the eggs. Have the bunny and the eggs gather at their starting points. To play, bunny begins by calling out colors. As soon as he calls a player's color, that egg takes off through the course, with the bunny in pursuit. If the bunny manages to tag the egg before he can make it back to their home base, the players swap places and the eggs all select new colors. If not, the bunny tries with a new color.

Wacky Tag

One person is "it." He calls out a random style of movement (walking on all fours, hopping like a frog). Everyone must move about accordingly. Each new player tagged "it" names the new movement, and the game continues.

Paper Chase

Players line up across one end of the room. Hand each person two sheets of newspaper; they must stand on one sheet and hold the other. On go, each player quickly sets the sheet he is holding on the ground in front of him and steps onto it with both feet. He then picks up the first page, sets it in front, and continues until he reaches the finish line.

Twenty-One

One person stands by the basketball hoop, while the other takes a shot from the foul line. If he makes it, he earns two points and continues shooting from the line. If he misses, both players try to grab the rebound and make a basket. Whoever makes a basket earns one point and becomes the next foul shooter. The first to earn exactly twenty-one points wins.

Frolf (Frisbee Golf)

Set up a golf course and play frisbee around the course.

Turning Heads

A quarter and a basketball are all you'll need to play this fun summertime challenge for two. Chalk a row of three large, equal-sized squares on a playing surface and place a quarter in the center of the middle square. Have the players stand in the two end squares and take turns aiming the basketball at the coin. They earn one point each time they hit the coin, and two points if they flip it over. The first to score eleven points wins.

Corner Kicks

Mark off a square playing area and have one player go to the center. Each of the three remaining players stand in a different corner. The person with the ball kicks it to a player in one of the other corners. The corner players continue kicking the ball back and forth, while the player in the middle attempts to steal it en route. If the middle player steals the ball, the player who kicked the ball is now in the center.

Skellzies

Draw a playing field on a sidewalk square. The numbers one, six, five and two are in the corners; the number eight is in the top middle square; the middle side squares are three and four; the bottom middle square is seven; and the center square is the number nine. Place bottle caps on the ground and flick them into the numbered squares, beginning with the number one. Upon making "onesies," players must shoot for "twosies." The number nine is poison, and you lose three turns for landing there. The first person to make it though eight numbers wins.

Amoeba

Players must work together to navigate a course like an amoeba. First, determine a course for the group to follow, and a finish line. Divide into two teams—not quite half and half. Have the larger group join hands in a snug, outward facing circle around the smaller group. Adjust the sizes of the groups if necessary, and then select one player in the inner circle to be the nucleus. At the cue, the nucleus begins directing the whole group through the course by calling out instructions, such as step to your right, back up two steps. Players cannot move until the nucleus instructs them to. The game ends when all of the players have completed the course.

Barefoot Boccie

Each player removes one sock, balls it up, and labels it with tape. Set a hat or bowl as a target on one side of the room and mark a tossing line on the other. Players then take turns standing at the line on one foot trying to toss their sock into the target. Whoever succeeds gets one point. The first person to score five points wins.

Ghost In the Graveyard

One player (the ghost) hides. The other players stay together at the base and count loudly in unison to twenty, at which point they all head off to search for the hiding ghost. When a seeker spots the ghost, he yells, "Ghost in the graveyard," and along with everyone else, runs back toward base. The ghost lets out a scream and chases after the seekers, trying to tag as many as he can before they all reach base.

Guts

Two lines of players face off forty-five feet apart and wing the frisbee back and forth, getting points for each catch or for each throw the other team can't handle. First team to earn twenty-one points wins.

Frisbee Boccie

Toss a tennis ball into the yard, and take turns trying to land a frisbee as close to it as possible. A player who manages to land a throw directly on the ball automatically wins that round, otherwise the closest throw wins. Each win scores one point, and you can play to any score you choose.

Super Sock Toss

Fill socks with one cup of sand and tie off the open end. Each player will need three socks. Use rocks to form two two-foot rings about ten feet apart, each with a single rock in the center. Players take turns standing at one ring and tossing their socks underhand to the other. They earn five points for each sock they land inside the ring and ten if the sock comes to rest on the center rock. First player to fifty points wins.

Royal Kings

This is a cross between handball and four square. You need a row of four-foot squares alongside a building, and a playground ball, such as a kickball. Starting with the left most square, mark it with an ace, then king, queen and so on. You need one square per player. The player in the ace square begins the game by hitting the ball with his hand so that it bounces in his own square, hits the wall, and ricochets into another player's square. That player hits the ball in the same manner. Play continues until someone misses the ball or fails to hit it as required. That player then earns a letter to try and spell *kings*, and moves to the far right end of the line. The other players move left and the person in the ace square serves again. A player is out when he has earned all the letters in the word *kings*.

Knockout

Players line up single file behind the free throw line. The first person starts by shooting a free throw. If he sinks it, he goes to the end of the line and stays in the game. If he misses, he must quickly rebound it and put it in before the next person in line makes his shot.

One Team Volleyball

You will need a ball, and a string tied between two trees. Everyone stands on the same side of the string. One player begins by hitting the ball into the air above the group, and quickly scoots under the net to the other side. One by one, the remaining players follow suit, hitting the ball into the air and slipping under the net to the other side, where the whole process begins again.

King of the Dribblers

Everyone gets a ball. Players must stay inside a designated playing area and dribble; no standing around. As they bounce the ball, they try to knock everyone else's ball away with their free hand. The last player dribbling is crowned king or queen.

Horse

Players take shots from anywhere around the court. If one player makes a shot, the other must duplicate it. If he misses he gets a letter. The first player to spell *horse* loses.

Soccer Dodgeball

Played like dodgeball, but instead of throwing the ball you kick it.

Driveway Bowling

Set up two empty cans approximately two feet apart and several feet in front of your garage door. From a starting line down the driveway, try to bowl a playground ball through the cans without knocking them down. If you succeed, you score two points. If you knock down one can, your score one point.

Smaug's Jewels

Smaug the dragon tries to protect his jewels (a bandanna) from the thieves. He cannot touch the bandanna but can stand right over it if he wants. The thieves dart and dive around Smaug trying to steal the jewel without Smaug tagging them. Those tagged are frozen like statues forever. If a thief succeeds in stealing the jewels, he becomes Smaug and a new round begins.

Chicken Challenge

Players pair off, each tucking a bandanna into his back pocket. On "go," both players in each pair begin hopping on one foot, and flapping one arm like a wing. Each uses his free hand to attempt to steal his opponent's bandanna while maneuvering to keep his own from being snatched. The first player in each pair to lose his bandanna or his balance is out. Players are also forbidden to set their foot down.

Sardines

Select one person to be the hider. He picks a place to hide while the rest of the group closes their eyes and counts to fifty. Then everyone splits up to look for him. As each player finds the hiding place, he quietly joins the hider until everyone is squashed in together. The player who found the hider first gets to be the hider in the next round. This can also be played in the dark, with flashlights.

Sticker Tag

Each person gets at least six stickers. Everyone scatters to different areas of the yard. On the count of three, players must try to tag one another with a sticker, ideally without getting stuck themselves. You can't tag the same player twice in a row. You can't pull stickers off your own body to put on someone else. You can designate a tree or other area as a base. Once everyone has used up all their stickers, the game is over. The person with the fewest stickers on them wins.

Noodle Toss

Hang a hula hoop from a tree. Give each player a pool noodle, and place him several paces away from the hoop. Challenge each child to throw the noodle through the hoop; each time he succeeds, he takes a step back. The player who is the farthest away from the hoop and still makes his mark wins.

JUMP ROPE GAMES

- *Fortune Teller.* As you jump, ask the rope a question about your life. To see into your future, say one of your possible answers each time you jump the rope. The word you are saying when you miss is your answer.
- *Double Dutch.* Two turners twirl two long ropes. One rope's up while the other's down.
- *Under the Moon.* The player runs under the rope without skipping.
- *Rocking the Cradle.* When you sway the rope from side to side rather than over the head.
- *Crossie.* Solo jumper crosses arms when jumping and then uncrosses her arms.
- *Peppers.* Turn the rope as fast as possible. Say "hot" and go even faster.

CIRCLE GAMES

Flee the Country

Everyone stands in a big circle. One person in the middle of the circle will call out different positions, such as "bull fight." Everyone in the circle has to try to get into that position with someone else as fast as possible. The last person to form that position is eliminated from the game. Continue until there is just one person left in the circle. Some positions ideas:

- *Flee the Country*: Jump out of the circle as fast as you can.
- *Bull Fight*: Two people together, one is the bull and the other the bull fighter.
- *Eiffel Tower*: Two people will stand in an upside down *V* with hands touching at the top.
- *Royal Throne*: Three people get together. Two clasp hands and form a chair and the other person sits in the "chair."
- *Tea Party*: Four people gather and pretend to drink a cup of tea.

Oink

The object of the game is to pass a snort around the circle as fast as you can without laughing. Sit in a circle facing in. One person snorts at the person next to him. The snort continues around the circle in the same way. You may not laugh when you are snorting or being snorted at; if you do, you are out of the circle. Continue eliminating until two people are left; they have a snort off until one of them laughs.

Newspaper Bop Game

Choose a theme for the game. Each person chooses an object from that theme. Roll up a newspaper. One person is in the middle and holds the newspaper they call out something from the theme. The person who chose that item from the theme must call out another item in that theme before the person in the middle bops them with the newspaper. The person who chose that item must call out something else before he gets hit. The person in the middle tries to bop each person before they have a chance to call out another item from the theme.

For example, if the theme is fruit and you chose apple, when the person in the middle calls out apple, you must call out another fruit (banana, grape, orange) before he hits you with the newspaper. If you call out banana, the person who chose banana must call out another fruit before he gets hit, and so forth.

Grunt Piggy Grunt

Everyone sits in a circle. The person who is "it" is blindfolded and holds a pillow. That person goes to someone in the circle and puts the pillow on his lap, sits on it, and says, "Grunt piggy, grunt." The blindfolded person then tries to guess whose lap they are on. If he guesses right, that person whose lap he was sitting on is now "it."

Thimble Game

You will need a glass of water and a thimble. Pick a topic. Fill the thimble with water. The person who is "it" holds the thimble of water. That person then chooses in their mind something that fits the topic. Go around the circle and the one who says what "it" is thinking gets the thimble of water thrown at them, and then they are "it."

The Big Wind Blows

All but one player (the caller) sit arm's length apart in a circle. The caller stands in the middle and begins the game by saying, "The big wind blows…" and completes the sentence with a description that applies to himself and to at least two other members of the group. All the players to whom that description applies must get up and sit in another seat. The player without a seat becomes the caller for the next round.

Find the Coin

Sit in a circle with one person in the middle. The other players pass a coin slyly around the circle. The person in the middle says stop when he thinks he knows where the coin is. He will now try to guess who has the coin. If guessed right, the players then switch places.

Ringer

You will need a piece of chalk and assorted marbles. Chalk a five-foot diameter ring on a smooth, flat surface. Mark two lines touching opposite edges of the ring (lag and pitch lines). In the center, draw two crossed lines and arrange thirteen target marbles along them. Each player will need a shooter marble. The player whose shooter lands closest to either side of the lag line goes first. With each turn, a player attempts to knock the target marbles out of the ring, shooting from anywhere outside the circle. If he succeeds, he earns one point for each marble knocked out and goes again. If he misses or his shooter rolls out of the ring, his turn is over.

Chop the Chocolate

Sit in a circle and place a large unwrapped candy bar on a plate with a knife and fork. Next to the plate, put a pile of crazy clothes. Roll a die. If that player gets anything other than a six, he passes the die along. When someone rolls a six, he must dress in the crazy clothes and chop off pieces of the candy bar. Whatever he can chop off, he can eat. As soon as the next six comes along, that person gets to dress and chop the chocolate. When the candy bar is gone, the game is over.

Sucking M&M's

Each person gets a straw. Fill a bowl with M&M's. Pass a pie tin around with two dice in it. Start rolling the dice. When doubles are rolled, that person gets to start sucking M&M's out of the bowl and the dice keep going around the circle. When doubles are rolled again, that person grabs the bowl and starts sucking M&M's. Play this game for five minutes and count up how many M&M's each person has.

Wet Feet

Play like musical chairs. Lay newspaper pieces out on the ground, representing dry ground. When the music plays, all players walk around the newspapers. When the music stops, all players need to get on dry ground. Continue removing newspapers. It is fun to see how many people you can fit on one newspaper.

Block Tower

Gather a pile of blocks. Players sit in a circle around the blocks, adding blocks to a tower one at a time. The round is over with the tower collapses.

Circle the Circle

The group forms a circle and holds hands. Place two large hoops together between two people resting on their grasped hands. See how quickly the participants in the circle can cause the hoops to travel around the circle (over the people) in opposite directions, through each other, and back to the originating point. It is interesting to see what the group's response is when you ask who won. It takes some thought to realize that the entire group was working together as a team—no losers, no winners.

Foxes and Squirrels

Stand in a circle. The foxes (two tennis balls) are passed quickly around the circle, as in a game of hot potato. Squirrels, (nerf ball) get tossed around at the same time. As in dodgeball, you're out if the squirrel ball tags you, but the thrower is out if you catch it. You have to be ready to receive and pass the two fox balls going around in the circle.

If You Love Me Baby, Smile

Player sits on lap of another player and says their name and then repeats three times "I love you baby but I just can't smile." The player that says this can't smile or then this person is automatically in the center and proceeds to follow the routine.

EDUCATIONAL GAMES

Shadows on the Wall

Turn off the lights. Turn on a flashlight. Hide behind a chair or a couch. Now tell a story while using your hands to cast shadow creatures on the wall. Let your imagination go wild.

Speed Scrabble

Leave the scrabble board in the box and place all the letters facedown on a table. Each player draws five tiles. At "go" players use their tiles to form a word, creating their own personal scrabble grids. The first player to make a word shouts "go," and everyone grabs another two tiles, whether they've completed a word or not. The person who uses all his tiles first is the winner.

Happy Memory Game

Make about forty cards, one subject per card. Include locations you have been as a family. Each person draws a card and has three minutes to say a happy memory that corresponds with the subject on the card. In the second round, you need to come up with two happy memories, three memories in the third round, and so forth.

Waiting Game

Write the letters of the alphabet in a column down one side of a piece of paper, then write the first twenty-six letters of a line from a song, poem, or saying in a second column so that you have two letters on each line. Now see what two word phrases, silly sayings, or even famous names you can think of for each pair of initials.

Math-o

Make bingo cards that say "Math-o." Write *free* in the center space and fill the first column with five numbers between one and six. Fill the second column with five numbers between seven and twelve, and so on. Make squares to pull out of a box that have equations that add, subtract, multiply, or divide to get the answer one through six. (For example: M 2+4 or T 15-14). Give each person a card, and small cereal or jelly beans for markers. The caller picks an equation from the box and players search for a match on their card. The first player to cover a row is the winner.

Spelling for Dollars

Pick a word for your child to spell. After spelling the first word correctly, give your child a penny. For each subsequent turn, either he can bank his change and spell the next word right for another penny, or he can gamble all or part of his stash in a double or nothing bid. If he spells the next word correctly he gets four pennies. If he misspells, he loses two pennies. Have lifelines available, such as one dictionary consultation, ask a parent, or fifty-fifty where only two options are available. This can be good incentive to do homework.

Memory

Make concentration cards with stickers, magazine pictures, letters, numbers, or computer clip art. Turn the cards over and see who can get the most matches.

Human Typewriter

Assign each member of the team a different letter. As questions are asked, answers must be spelled out by having the people arrange themselves in order of spelling the word.

Spelling Baseball

To play, divide into two teams and instead of pitching balls, announce words for each person "at bat" to spell. If the batter spells the word correctly, he gets on base, but if the batter misspells the word, it's an out. More difficult words are worth a double or a triple, or even a homerun.

Par 20

Using only the number cards from a deck, deal five cards to each player and place the rest of the deck facedown as the draw pile. Starting left of the dealer, players try to make a mathematical equation totaling twenty from any three of their five cards. If you can't make an equation that totals exactly twenty, your score for that round is the difference. Play five rounds; the lowest score wins.

Good Morning Madame

You will need two decks of cards. Deal all the cards. Players take turns laying their top card (without looking) face up in the middle of the table. If a number card is turned up, play proceeds to the person on the left. If it is an ace, king, queen, or jack, all players must respond as follows:

- *Ace*: Slap the card with your hand
- *King*: Offer a salute
- *Queen*: Sing out, "Good morning, madame"
- *Jack*: Shout, "Boo!"

The first person to execute the correct move takes the entire pile of cards. Whoever collects all the cards first wins the game.

LINE GAMES

Gum Game

You will need oven mitts, a knife, a fork, some gum, and dice for this game. Place a pack of gum in the middle of a circle. Roll two dice and if the number adds up to seven, put on the mitts, and use the knife and fork, to open the gum before the next person rolls a seven. See how many pieces of gum you can get in your mouth before a set time is up. You could do this with other objects in the middle such as a present, or candy bar.

Pass It On

Sit close together in two lines facing the same direction. The person in the front of each line rolls a die. When one of them gets a six, both of them pass a small object to the person behind them who passes it on until it reaches the end. When it gets to the last person, that person must get up and race to the front of the line with the object and sit down. The person who sits down first gets to sit in the front of the line. The person who was second goes back to his spot.

Shuffle Caps

Create a scoring triangle on a table with tape. The tip of the triangle is worth fifty points, the middle is worth twenty-five points, and the base is worth ten points. Use another piece of tape to mark the push-off point. Take turns sliding your caps (milk bottle lids, flat side down) from behind the push-off point. More than half the cap must be inside the space to count as in. The first player to score 200 points is the winner. If you shoot your cap off the table, you lose twenty-five points, but if you knock an opponent's cap, he loses twenty-five points.

Marble Cliff Hanger

Two players sit at the far ends of a rug and take turns shooting marbles (they each get six) toward the opposite side. In each round, whoever gets his marble closest to the edge without it rolling off gets a point.

Bean Pitch

Each participant gets ten beans to try to pitch into a bottle. The kid with the greatest number of successful tosses wins the game.

TRAVELING GAMES

Eating the Alphabet

First player says, "I'm so hungry, I could eat…" and says something starting with the letter *A*. The second player adds a tasty morsel starting with the letter *B*. Continue on through the alphabet.

License Plate Games

- Make phrases out of letters in license plates.
- Search for ABCs.
- Play license plate twenty-one. Each person picks a license plate and adds up numbers; the plate closest to twenty-one wins.

Poodle

In this game, the word *poodle* is substituted for a verb. To play, one child picks a secret verb; then the other kids ask questions using poodle in place of the verb, such as, Can you poodle in a pool?, Does poodling make you tired?, and so forth. The child who guesses the secret verb correctly gets to choose the next one.

The Name Game

Link famous people by the letters of their names. The first player picks someone famous such as George Washington. The next player picks a celebrity whose first name begins with the same letter as the previous person's last name, such as Whitney Houston, and so forth.

Scavenger Hunt

Make a master list with several of each item on it, such as six motels, twenty-two red cars, and so forth. Work together to find all the items on the list.

Radio Bingo

Draw a grid on a piece of paper and write a word in each box that is likely to be heard on the radio. Listen to the radio and mark the appropriate boxes, until they get bingo.

Games-to-Go Bag

Pack a bag of travel games that are designated for trips only, such as Boggle, Simon, and Yahtzee. Go to www.areyougame.com for more travel games.

Backseat I Spy

Write a list of items that you might see on your trip. Hand out the lists and challenge your kids to see how many of the items they can spot before you reach your destination.

To the Letter

One person begins by stating a category, and a number of letters, and then naming an appropriate item. For example, he might pick the category of animals and the number three, then say "cow." Players take turns coming up with three-letter animals until everyone is stumped. The player who contributed the last word wins the round and starts the next one.

Backseat Boredom Buster

Make a magnetic board with a baking sheet covered with plain contact paper to serve as a drawing board. Then affix pieces of magnetic tape to dry erase markers. For an eraser, tightly tie one end of a piece of ribbon to a small cloth and the other end to the hole in the baking sheet handle. Make several games like bingo, checkerboard, crossword puzzles, tic tac toe, and so forth. Create a storage place for all the games by attaching a file folder to the back of the baking sheet.

The Car Next Door

Create stories about the passengers in the car next to yours. What is each person's profession? What is each person's favorite food? Where are they going? Be creative. Include details such as their names and favorite hobbies.

RELAYS

Balloon Platoon

Divide players into pairs that stand back to back with elbows linked. Hand one child in each pair an inflated balloon. On cue, the teams try their best to reach the finish line, transfer the balloon from one partner to the other with their arms still linked, and be the first to return to the start.

Sneaker Relay

Divide into teams and set up a box across from each team at the far end of an area. On cue, the first person in each group races to his team's box, removes and deposits his shoes, and runs back to tag the next person. The game continues until the last teammate in line has thrown his shoes in the box and has run back to the starting line. At that point, the first person races back to the box to retrieve his shoes and put them on before retagging the next person, and so on. The team to complete both parts of the relay first, wins.

Panty Hose Polo

Cut a pair of panty hose up the middle and drop an orange or tennis ball into the toe of each leg. Stick two lengths of tape to the floor about fifteen feet apart for the start and finish lines. Place two more oranges or tennis balls behind the start line. Tie the panty hose legs around two players' waists so that the oranges hang about a half inch off the floor. Without using their hands, players must swing the panty hose orange or tennis ball to knock their floor orange or tennis ball over the finish line and back. First team to complete the course wins.

Spoon Relay

The object of this relay is to have the biggest piles of dried beans at the end of a three-minute block of time. For each team, place a bowl filled with dried beans at the starting line, then set a grocery-sized paper bag twenty feet from each bowl. When the race begins, the first person on each team uses a wooden spoon to scoop up beans from the bowl and then races off to dump them in the bag. Then he hands the spoon off to the next person who follows suit, and so on, until the time is up. The team with the most beans in the bag wins.

Hula Hoop Relay

Divide into teams and have them form two straight lines facing each other from opposite ends of the playing area. In the middle of the space between each team, have someone hold up a hula hoop. The first person in one line runs through the hula hoop to the other line of people. He grabs the hand of the first person in line, and the two of them run again through the hula hoop back to the first line, where another person joins them and so on until the whole team is hand in hand and they all run through the hoop.

Lemon Derby

Each contestant must use a stick to roll a lemon to the finish line. One possible variation is to use a water bottle filled halfway with water, or use a hula hoop and roll it with a stick.

Suitcase Relay

Pack two suitcases with the same number of clothes. When given the cue, the first person on each team picks up the suitcase and runs to the designated point. He dresses in the clothes, runs back to the starting line, undresses, and closes the suitcase. The next person then does the same thing. Continue until the last person is back at the starting line.

TEAMWORK GAMES

Human Bracelet

Two teams stand facing each other. Each team has a ball of yarn with a spoon tied to one end. The first member has to thread the spoon through his shirt without taking off his clothing. Then he passes the spoon to the next team member, who does the same thing, and so on. When everyone is connected, the teams send the spoon back, one by one, through their clothing until the first team member is again holding the spoon.

Take Your Seats

Participants stand in a circle, shoulder to shoulder, facing inward. Next, have everyone turn to the right and then simultaneously sit down on the knees of the person behind him. Players should sit slowly and carefully. It may take a couple of attempts, but it can be done!

Human Knot Game

Everyone stands in a circle and grabs two hands belonging to two different people. Then everyone tries to untangle the group.

You can also have everyone but one person join hands while facing the center of the circle. That person is the doctor. While the doctor is out of the room, everyone steps over each other, twists, turns, and basically turns the circle into a knot. No matter what, they can't let go of each others hands. When the circle is in a knot, call the doctor back in. The doctor then comes in and tries to make everyone face each other in a circle again, by unraveling the knot without unlinking any hands.

Desert Island

Everyone on the team stands on the Island (a rug). Tell them they cannot step off the island, because of sharks. Without stepping off the island, they need to turn the rug over.

Balance Beam

Make a beam that is ten to twelve inches off the ground. Each team must stand on the beam. Without speaking they will need to change position on the beam and go from oldest to youngest by birthday. No one can step off the beam, and no one can speak. If any clothing or body parts touch the ground the group must start over.

Plug The Sieve

Get two five-gallon buckets and drill holes all around the bottom and sides of it. You will also need four five-gallon buckets with no holes. Fill two of the buckets with water. Put the other two buckets at the end of the relay. Each team will dump the water into the bucket with the holes and then run down to the two empty buckets and drop the water that is left into it. Measure each team's water level. The object is to work together to plug all the holes so that you can have the most water in the end.

Honesty Web

Prepare a web by criss-crossing yarn back and forth and up and down between two trees to form a giant spider web. The openings in the web must be large enough for a person to fit through them. There must be more openings in the web than there are members of the team. The object is to have all team members pass through the web without touching the rope. Each team can help their team members by lifting them through the holes. When one member passes through an opening, it cannot be passed through again.

Lean on Me

The object of this activity is to have two players stand up from a seated position without using their hands. Have the two players sit back to back on the floor, each with his knees bent in front of him, and arms folded across his chest. On cue, the players attempt to stand up together.

WATER GAMES

Cold Feet

Fill a child's swimming pool with buckets of ice cubes. Using only their feet, participants see how many ice cubes they can get in a bucket in five minutes.

Sit on It

Fill twenty-four balloons with water. Load two buckets with a dozen balloons each and place them at one end of your yard. Divide the kids into two teams and position them at the other end of the yard. On cue, the first player on each team races to the bucket and grabs a balloon and sits on it until it pops. The team that pops all of their balloons first wins.

Water Olympics
- Set up a high water jump
- Launch a jump rope splash (hold a cup of water while jumping rope)
- Do a water balloon toss
- Do the water limbo
- Fill sponges with water and then race to a bucket and squeeze the water in to fill up the bucket.
- Pair up and make it from one point to another without using hands, holding a water balloon between each pair's shoulders

Rainy Relay

Divide into two teams. Provide each team with two buckets, one empty and one full of water, as well as a plastic cup with three holes punched into the sides. Set the empty buckets at one end of the yard and the full ones at the other. On cue, the first player on each team dips his cup into his water and holds it over his head as he dashes to the other end of the yard. Players are not allowed to cover the holes with their fingers. When a player reaches the second bucket, he dumps what is left in his cup into it. The game continues until the formerly full bucket is empty. The team with the most water in the second bucket wins.

Water Balloon Volleyball

Using towels and water balloons, play volleyball. Divide into two teams of four. Each person holds one corner of the towel and volleys the balloon to the other side. The other team tries to catch the balloon in their towel without it breaking.

Mommy Polo

Played in the pool like Marco Polo. Kids yell "mommy" and moms say "polo."

Swimming Pool Relay

- Swim across the pool pushing a beach ball with your nose
- Paddle across the pool with water noodles as fast as you can
- Do the breaststroke with rubber ducks on your head

You can come up with other fun tasks to complete; the first team to complete all the different laps is the winner.

Sponge Brigade

Divide the players into two teams and have the members of each team lie down side by side, alternating directions: first person head up, second person head down, and so forth. Place a bucket of water near the head of each line. For each team, soak a large sponge in the water, then have the first player on each team hold it with her feet. On cue, the teams pass their sponges down the line and back using only their feet to move it from player to player. The person at the head of the line returns it to the bucket. If a player drops the sponge, he may sit up to recover it, but must use only his feet to get it back into the game.

A Family Book

Great Moments to be Remembered

In our families, it is important to create a sense of belonging, and a knowledge that no matter what changes outside our home, there are people whose love will never change.

"There is something to the notion of 'contact comfort' . . . that occurs in a healthy family . . . there is nothing quite like being able to come home at night [to a] loving, supporting family [who let you know] 'You're going to be okay,' or 'Way to go!' . . . This is what happens when you're in the presence of people who love you for who you are—nothing more, nothing less" (Dew, Sheri, *If Life Were Easy, It Wouldn't be Hard, and other Reassuring Truths* [Salt Lake City: Deseret Book, 2005], 78-79).

A family book provides a tangible object where you gather important information for your family to look at and live by. They can see how they fit in, and why they belong.

A family book is a place for current family records, goals, dreams, organization, and accomplishments. Your family book is your own collection of the things that make your family unique.

This chapter contains ideas for ten sections of a family book. Because your family is unique, make your book fit your family. The sections provided are ideas that can be changed to fit the needs of your family.

SECTION 1: A FAMILY MISSION STATEMENT

A mission statement states the purpose for which the organization was created. It represents vision, commitment, focus, and is the plan to fulfill this purpose. A mission statement is typically written in one sentence. To write a mission statement: Sit down with every member of your family. Each person should write down ideas and suggestions to answer the questions:

- What is the purpose of our family?
- How do we plan to fulfill this purpose?

Write several statements about your family. Begin each statement with "we believe . . ." List strengths and weaknesses of your family, beginning with strengths. Address each of the strengths and weaknesses. Do this activity with sincere intent, and really listen to each person's suggestions. Write down ideas of what you envision your family to be like in the future. Write down dreams and goals. Come up with a mission statement using the information you have discussed.

Once you have written your mission statement, post it in your home in a place where it can be seen. Discuss this often, and remind each family member that he has a part in the mission statement. (Anderson, Angelle. "Creating a Gospel Centered Home." Campus Education Week. Brigham Young University, Provo. August 2000).

SECTION 2: YOUR FAMILY STORY

This section is a page or two about how your family began. Include how you felt about each other on the first date and go on until the engagement and marriage. Continue the story with the birth of each child, your jobs, your homes, your cars. Write down memories of each stage of your life. Include documents like a copy of your marriage certificate, birth certificates, and other special keepsakes.

SECTION 3: SPOTLIGHT SECTION

Make a tab for each person in your family. Put important papers for each person in their section. Make up a spotlight form for each person in your family to fill out. Information on this sheet should include favorite food, places to visit, song, storybook, things to do, friends, and heroes. Write down their S.T.O.R.Y:

- S is for strengths. Each person should write down five strengths.
- T is for topic. Have each person write down five things he is good at.
- O is for optimal conditions. Each person should write down what gets him excited, and what keeps him going.
- R is for relationships. Have each person think about what role he plays in relationships with others. Do you want everyone to follow you? Do you only ask for help if you need it? Do you like

to work on things with others? Or, do you just want others to tell you what to do, and you'll do it?

- *Y* is for "yes!" Think about what makes you happy and excited. What is most satisfying to you?

(Lucado, Max, *Cure for the Common Life* [Nashville: W Publishing Group, 2005], 35-39).

You could have each person write down a favorite saying or motto for the year. Include a small picture of each person with this form.

SECTION 4: GOALS

Each year write down family goals in the following areas:

- *Physical.* Learn a new sport, or make an exercise goal.
- *Mental.* Learn a new game, or read a good book.
- *Social.* Make a new friend, plan a party, or practice smiling more.
- *Spiritual.* Memorize a scripture, attend church weekly, and pray.
- *Educational.* Be more organized with school, and improve study habits.

Each month, go over the goals and see how well you are progressing. Each member of the family should also make personal goals. If goals are written down, it is more likely they will be accomplished.

SECTION 5: PIE NIGHT

PIE stands for "personal interview and evaluation." The first Sunday of each month, meet individually with each child and interview them.

- Record the date of the interview.
- Write down any concerns that they may have.
- Make note of areas that they need to work on.
- Recognize good things that they have been doing.
- Go over their family responsibility and change their responsibility each month.
- Write down things that have happened since the last PIE night.
- Write down things they have going on in the coming month.
- Calendar a date for one on one time with a parent.
- Have them choose meals that they would like to eat one night of each week for the month.
- Begin and end this interview with a prayer, and eat pie!

Ideas for Family Responsibilities:

- *Education.* This family member will be responsible for organizing family nights for the month. He can choose what topic he would like to learn about.

- *Service.* This family member will be organizing service projects that the whole family will participate in for the month.
- *Activities.* This family member plans activities that he would like to do during the month. He needs to plan how to carry out the activities.
- *Unity.* This family member makes eating dinner together, family prayer, and scripture study a priority. He will schedule these family times, and make sure other family members are present.
- *Order.* This family member is in charge of the job chart each week. He will rotate jobs and think of creative ways to get the jobs done.
- *Sunshine.* This family member is in charge of making others happy. He will freely give hugs and kisses, write thank-you notes, and bring smiles to the family the whole month long.

You could come up with other responsibilities to meet the needs of your family. When each person has a responsibility, it takes the pressure off Mom and Dad. Rotating the responsibilities will also help.

Make an interview form and keep the completed forms in the family book. It is good to review the last interview and see how well each child has progressed over the month (Anderson, Angelle. "Creating a Gospel Centered Home." Campus Education Week. Brigham Young University, Provo. August 2000).

SECTION 6: NOTABLE MEMORIES

Throughout the year write little notes of good things that happen in your family. Put the notes in a jar and on New Year's Day read all the notes to remember your past year. Place all the notes in an envelope and then place them in the section of the book for notable memories.
This section should also include a journal.

Make a tab for awards and accomplishments in this section also. This is a good place to put report cards, certificates, ribbons, and mementos.

SECTION 7: OUR YEAR IN REVIEW

Each person in your family should answer the following questions each year:

- What was your greatest accomplishment this year?

- What was your favorite vacation this year?
- What was the hardest thing you did this year?
- What is your favorite saying or phrase?
- What is your favorite TV show?
- What was the best movie this year?
- Who are some of your friends?
- What is your best memory from this year?
- What is your worst memory from this year?
- What is the most touching moment from this year?
- What is the biggest change that happened to you this year?
- What was your worse sickness or illness this year?

Make a scrapbook page for each person using the answers to the questions. Put the scrapbook pages in the "year in review" section behind a tab with the year written on it.

SECTION 8: FAMILY LISTS

This section should have wish lists for each family member. This should be a place to write down dreams and goals for the future. When someone in your family mentions something that they want, write it down. Take the lists when you go shopping; they will make shopping so much easier! Include personal information such as shoe size, clothes size, color swatches of room decorations, and other gift ideas.

Write down items that the family would like to buy. Make a plan for saving money to purchase these items. Write the things you want the most and a plan for going about getting these things.

SECTION 9: CHRISTMAS LETTERS

Keep newsletters and Christmas cards that you send out year after year. This is a good way to keep track of what your family was up to throughout the years. It is also fun to keep your family Christmas pictures year after year and see how much your family changes.

SECTION 10: FAMILY NIGHT

Make a list of topics your family would like to learn about. And make a schedule of family-night activities. Use a form to give out assignments for family night, such as conducting, opening prayer, lesson or scripture, activity, song, treat, and closing prayer. Fill in a family member's name by each job and keep track of what each family member does each week so you can rotate responsibilities.

Extended Family Network

Keeping Family Ties Strong

One of the most important assets children need to succeed is to have a good relationship with adults who are not their parents. Grandparents, aunts, and uncles are great candidates for these adults. If children feel they can go to their grandparents, aunts, or uncles when problems come up, they will feel more secure in life. Children need to feel that they are important. What better way to show them than to spend time together as a family.

This section provides many examples for extended party activities, grandparent tips, and ways to stay connected with extended family.

GRANDPARENT MEMORY MAKERS

Keep a file of ideas to use as a reference when you need something to do. Time with grandchildren should be full of fun, love, and memories. Be genuinely interested in the things they care about. When they have a game or other performance, make an effort to attend.

Keep a game closet in your house, stocked with games, toys, balls, and books. Take your grandchildren out to lunch for their birthday. Take pictures of them with their mom; she is usually the one taking the picture and will be left out of many of their childhood pictures.

GRANDPARENT GIFTS OF LOVE

- Have sleepovers on holidays and birthdays. Organize a camping trip with all the grandkids.
- Make cookies during the Christmas holidays and organize projects for their parents.

- Read to your grandchildren and teach them to love books.
- Write letters to those who do not live close.

GRANDPARENT GIFTS OF HERITAGE
- Learn about the countries where your ancestors came from and have a theme party about those countries.
- Take old home movies or pictures and put them on a DVD, with music, for them to watch.
- Tape record interviews with older relatives and transcribe them.
- Pass on a china set or heirloom on special birthdays.
- Make family calendars that include everyone's birthdays.
- Tell your grandchildren stories about you.
- Organize a family reunion and get them to help you with the planning.

GRANDPARENT GIFTS OF CREATIVITY
- Help them write a book.
- Frame a picture they have drawn for you.
- Gather creative toys, crafts, and activities you can do together.
- Calendar a monthly family time.

GRANDPARENT GIFTS OF LEARNING
- Read good books together. Give them a personalized book by writing a message to them in the front cover.
- Purchase several family-oriented films for them to watch at your house.
- Teach your grandchildren about nature. Go on nature walks and gather treasures.
- Let them teach you how to use the computer.
- Teach them basic cooking, cleaning, and organizing skills.
- Invite them to come to your home to set up for a family party.

GRANDPARENT GIFTS OF SELF-WORTH
- Make photo albums for each grandchild. Be sure to include pictures of them with you.
- Go around the room and tell one good thing about each person there.
- Purchase a journal for each grandchild. Write down how special they are to you.

- Participate in family tournaments such as ping-pong, bowling, and volleyball. Purchase a trophy that travels around with the winner until the next tournament.
- Encourage them to try out for parts in a play, sports teams, or to be an officer at their school. Let them know of your support.

FAMILY REUNION IDEAS

- *Raffles.* Every person attending contributes a present. Display all the presents on a big table and sell raffle tickets for $1.00 a piece. This helps cut the cost of the reunion.
- *Family Puzzle.* Create a puzzle with pictures of all the family members. The centerpiece should be a picture of the grandparents. Put the puzzle together at the reunion to see how everyone fits.
- *Family Flags.* Each family makes a flag that depicts their family. Spend time explaining what the symbols on the flag mean.
- *Name Tags.* Make name tags that include the family tree. On each name tag, have the person's name, and who his parents are.
- *T-shirts.* Design a T-shirt that everyone in the family wears at the reunion.
- *Family Auction.* Each family brings something to auction off. This can help cover some of the expenses of the reunion.
- *Pictures.* Take pictures of everyone in attendance; take group shots, generation shots, family pictures, and so forth. Put the pictures into a scrapbook.
- *Human Scavenger Hunt.* Make a list of descriptions of people at the reunion, such as "This person has twins." Everyone must go around and find the person who fits each description.
- *Video.* Each family makes a short video about life in their family. Put all the videos together and watch them.
- *Preserve Family History.* Before the reunion, ask each family to bring old photographs that they have. Make copies of these photos for everyone.
- *Holidays.* Put one family member in charge of each day. On the first day celebrate Valentines Day, the second day, Easter, the third day, Halloween, the fourth day Christmas, and the fifth day, throw a giant birthday party.
- *Dollar Store Bingo.* Purchase and wrap dollar store prizes. Play bingo and let the winners choose a prize from the dollar store gifts.

EXTENDED FAMILY PARTY THEMES

Plan the activities, food, decorations, and gifts, around the theme.

- *Jungle Expedition.* Name food crazy things, like snake eggs (grapes). Dress like you're going on an expedition. Play relay games with a jungle theme to them.
- *County Fair Carnival.* Play "Needle In a Haystack." Have a pig-calling contest and a watermelon seed spitting contest. Serve boxed lunches for dinner.
- *Sports Theme.* Set up your yard like a miniature golf course and have an area to play football. Serve refreshments like you would get at a ball game.
- *Water Theme.* Play pool games, sprinkler tag, play with water guns, and have rubber duck races. Serve hamburgers and ice cream cones.
- *Bake-Off.* Choose a food and have everyone bring their version of the food. Let the kids be the judges and decide on a winner.
- *Service.* Perform service for others; wash windows and cars, and do other random acts of service.
- *Easter Egg Hunt.* Do a color-coded egg hunt, search for prizes, decorate eggs, and serve a breakfast buffet.
- *Happy Birthday America.* Make red, white, and blue food. Have various activities and prizes for the winners.
- *Snow Day.* Have a snow sculpture contest and go sledding. Serve soup and hot chocolate to warm everyone up.
- *AFOOFA.* (All for one and one for all) Play teamwork games; tie everyone's hands together while eating dinner.

For more ideas, look to the monthly traditions in the chapter "Traditions That Build Unity." Many of those ideas can easily be adapted to parties with extended family members.

FAMILY NEWSLETTER

Assign one person to be in charge of the newsletter; each family sends in information about their activities from the last month. Send pictures, newspaper clippings, and artwork. Once everything is compiled, send the newsletter to everyone in the family.

FAMILY PICTURE WALL

Designate a wall in your home for pictures of extended family. Gather baby pictures of your parents, grandparents, aunts, and uncles. Include family pictures of each family.

FAMILY COOKBOOK

Recipes are powerful reminders of people, places, and good times. Gather favorite family recipes from all family members. Compile these recipes into a cookbook that all will treasure.

COUSIN PLACE MATS

Make place mats with pictures of cousins. Laminate them and let your child eat off them. This keeps their cousins in their minds all the time.

HOLIDAY CARE PACKAGES

Deliver care packages to extended family at each holiday.

SERVICE

Service opportunities provide an atmosphere to grow closer as a family, to do good things, and to have fun together all at the same time. Some service ideas:

- Prepare a skit and songs to perform at a rest home.
- Serve dinner at a homeless shelter.
- Go to the humane society and offer to walk or feed the dogs.
- Gather stuffed animals and donate them to your local fire department. (The fire department gives stuffed animals to kids who have to go for a ride in the ambulance.)
- Make kits for the children in the hospital. Include fun games, books, puzzles, and stuffed animals.
- Gather items to send to another country. Go through your clothes, toys, and other items and box them up for charity.
- Deliver meals to homebound people.
- Go on a service search. Divide into groups and give each group a time limit. See how much service each group can give in the time allotted.
- Make quilts to give to children who have been abused.
- Plan a fund-raiser such as a children's art gallery or a bake sale for you to earn money to give to your community or to a family in need.

The possibilities are endless and the feeling you get from providing worthwhile service is immeasurable.

EXTENDED FAMILY VACATIONS

Including extended family in vacations is a win-win situation. This is a great way to make memories. Before you go, choose a vacation that all ages would like. If you are planning activities, take a vote on what things your family would like to do. You can divide up during the day and meet back for dinner.

BINGO

Make cards with peoples' names on them. Draw the names out of a hat. The person whose name is drawn stands up so everyone can see who he is. This helps get to know names with faces.

HOMEMADE CHRISTMAS

Draw names with your extended family. Make rules such as the gift must be homemade and it cannot cost more than a set amount. You could give gifts of service, time together, homemade food, crafts, or letters. The goal is to really think about the person whose name you draw.

EXTENDED FAMILY SLEEPOVER

Plan a sleepover—parents included. Watch classic movies, have a board game tournament, eat snack food, and camp out on the floor. Enjoy each other's company!

Making Home A Haven

Home Is Where You Hang Your Heart

When you think of the ideal home, you think of a place where you feel safe and secure from the outside world. Home is a place where you can be yourself and feel accepted no matter what. Home should be a place where each member of the family wants to be.

In a national survey, men said that the thing they wanted most in their homes was tranquility. More than expensive furniture, a well-equipped garage, or a private study, they wanted peace and happiness at home.

Home should be a haven from the trials and conflicts of the outside world for every member of the family. It should be a place of acceptance and strength.

This section of the book will provide you with ideas to create a peaceful climate in your home, room by room. Helpful and practical household hints to make your home run smoothly, coupled with simple organizing tips, will allow you more time to spend time with your family.

KITCHEN AND DINING ROOM

The kitchen is a gathering place. When dinner is cooking, the aroma brings children into the kitchen. A must in the kitchen area is a table where you can sit and talk while eating, playing games, doing homework, and preparing meals.

Clutter can build up on the counters in the kitchen because that is where most paper ends up when it comes in the home. Develop a three-step filing system. The first folder should have things that need to be looked at. The second folder has things that need to be sent out, and the third folder has things that need to be put somewhere else. Go through your files once a week and clean them out. This will keep you on top of your paper clutter.

On your fridge, keep a list of items you need to buy. When you run out of something, write it on the list and the next time you go to the store you won't have to think of what it is that you just ran out of.

When the pantry is cluttered you waste precious time looking for things. You also waste money buying duplicates of things you already have.

When it comes to organizing your kitchen, ask yourself: What's working? What's not working? Why does clutter build up here? After you determine what is and is not working, make a plan. The plan should be your vision of what the finished product is. Sort through the cupboards; put all the cereal together, all the cans of soup together, and so forth. Buy containers that are clear so you can see what is in them. Label every container and the shelf it belongs on. Inform your family of the changes, and you will be amazed at how easy it is to keep this up.

Kitchen Tips
- To clean stove top, use vinegar or ammonia, and a sponge or paper towel.
- Cut a lemon in half and rub it over stove-top splatters and then simply wipe clean with a damp rag.
- Use diluted vinegar to remove soap film or other buildup on both white and colored stove tops as well as ceramic tiles.
- If you can't deal with a spill or boil-over immediately, sprinkle salt on the spill so it will easily clean up later. This also works for any food spills in your oven.
- Use an old toothbrush or a damp cotton swab with a bit of dishwashing liquid to clean push buttons and other small or hard-to-reach parts of the stove.
- Soak dirty knobs in hot water and dishwashing liquid (baking soda or ammonia works well too). Then use an old toothbrush to remove the now softened grime.
- Place an old towel soaked with ammonia on a flat baking pan and leave in a closed oven overnight. Remove pan and towel, and rinse out in the kitchen sink. Then use this dampened towel to wipe down the oven walls and racks.
- Use a cordless, handheld vacuum to pick up the white ash left in the bottom of a self-cleaning oven before wiping it out with a damp sponge.

- Clean the glass window in your oven door with a damp sponge and full strength vinegar. If the grease buildup is too heavy, use a razor blade to scrape it.
- Toothpaste works wonders on stubborn countertop stains.
- To clean a microwave, fill a bowl with water and sprinkle some Tang powder in the water. Microwave for five minutes. Wipe out with a damp rag.
- To clean a garbage disposal, put lemon slices, baking soda, and ice cubes down the disposal. Run the disposal for one minute and then wipe the sink.
- If you break a glass, press a slice of bread into the broken glass. The bread will pick up the small glass pieces.
- If you break an egg, pour salt on the egg and it will soak up the egg so you can scoop it right up.
- To get rid of fruit flies, take a glass and fill it up a half inch with apple cider and two drops dishwashing liquid; mix well. You will find those flies drawn to the cup, and gone forever.
- Get rid of ants! Put small piles of cornmeal where you see ants. They eat it and take it home, and can't digest it, so it kills them. It may take a week or so to see results, but it works!
- Before you pour sticky substances into a measuring cup, fill it with hot water. Dump out the hot water, but don't dry the cup. Next, add your ingredient, such as peanut butter, and watch how easily it comes out.
- Soak a cotton ball with almond extract and put it on the shelf in your fridge. Your fridge will smell fresh for a month!
- Lay the oven racks on your lawn overnight. The dew will combine with the enzymes in the grass to loosen any burned-on grease. Try it with your grill rack too.
- Put condiments in the fridge in a container for easier access.
- Before you go grocery shopping, clean out the fridge. Have a leftover dinner the night before and wipe all the fridge shelves so they will be ready for the new groceries.
- Remove frozen meats from the freezer at the first of the week. This way your meat will be ready to cook during the week.
- Spray your defrosted freezer with cooking spray. The next time you defrost it, it will be a cinch.

OFFICE AND COMMUNICATION CENTER

Organization and communication are huge factors toward making your home a haven. If you have a place where every member of the family can go to see what is on the schedule for the day, what is expected of them, and when and where everyone is, peace will reign in your home.

Communication resolves 80 percent of contention. To create a communication center, you should look at the needs of your family. Cork, magnet, and dry erase boards are all good materials to have in your communication center. Organize your board to the needs of your family. Some ideas include:

- Job charts
- Calendars
- Letters, announcements, and invitations
- Shopping list
- Menu
- Spotlight birthdays that are in the month
- Recognize awards and achievements
- A place for notes (So your kids can let you know where they are, when they will be home, and so forth.)
- Display your family mission statement
- Notable quotes
- A theme for every month of the year

Organize your office according to your needs. Make a schedule for bill paying, letter writing, and filing. Make sure that the papers and files you use the most are at the tip of your fingers. "A place for everything and everything in its place," is a good motto for your office. We live in the age of the Internet; we don't need to keep everything. If you have moved a paper three times, and it still doesn't have a place to go, get rid of it. Sort your mail before you come into the house. Keep a shredder by your garage door so you can shred anything with personal information and toss the junk mail so it doesn't even come into your home. Keep your bills to be paid in a folder, and when you receive bills put them straight into the folder. Write down dates of parties, weddings, and meetings on your calendar and then you can toss the invitations.

Paper doesn't have to take over your life. If you sort paper when it comes into the house and you have a place to put it, you will be amazed at how easy it is to overcome the paper piles.

Office Tips

- If you seal an envelope and then realize you forgot to include something inside, just place your sealed envelope in the freezer for an hour or two. Voila! It unseals easily.
- Label boxes or folders for each member of the family with *in* and *out*. Papers and assignments that need to be signed by a parent go in the *in* box; when signed and ready to go, put them in the *out* box.
- A good website for organizing and simplifying ideas and tips is www. getorganizednow.com.
- Immediately put store receipts in one section of your wallet. Once you get home, stash them all together in an envelope. For big ticket items, attach receipts to the warranty or instruction booklet.
- Open mail near a wastebasket and dump what you don't want as soon as it is opened.
- Avoid paying overdue fines for library books by writing their due date on your calendar.

MAKING JOBS FUN

- *Chore and More Jars.* In addition to regular chores, put amusing and fun tasks in the chore jar. Each person chooses one chore at a time. Work is all done when the jar is empty.
- *Kid of the Week.* For one week, one child is the "chosen child." That child gets to choose what TV shows to watch, what to have for dinner, and other extra privileges. Along with the extra privileges, give him chores.
- *Magic of Music.* Assign each person a chore. Put a song on and have them finish the job before the song ends.
- *Once-a-Week Pick Up.* Fill a basket with stray items during the week. Once a week, empty the basket and have everyone pitch in and put the items back where they belong.

LAUNDRY ROOM

Doing laundry is like a string of beads with no knot in the end. You will spend a lot of time in the laundry room; make it a pleasant place to be. Purchase a different color laundry basket for each member of your family. When you fold the laundry, put items into each member's basket for him to put away. Hang a pretend clothesline across one wall with miniature clothespins on it. Put a sign up that says, "Lost sole looking for a mate." When you find a mismatched sock, hang it on the line. This will make it easier to match when the other pair comes along.

Laundry Room Tips

- Clean your dryer lint collector by scrubbing in warm soapy water with a toothbrush at least every six months. This will increase the life of your dryer and speed up your drying time.
- Reduce static cling by pinning a safety pin to the seam of your clothing. Static cling will disappear!
- Gum can be dissolved and removed from hair and clothing by rubbing with peanut butter.
- Always dilute liquid bleach before adding to the wash. Otherwise, it weakens fibers.
- If the dryer stops and you aren't there, soak a wash cloth and add to clothes for five minutes to remove wrinkles.
- Make your own spray-and-wash. In a one-pint spray bottle, mix one-third cup liquid soap and one-third cup ammonia. Fill up with water the rest of the way. Apply to any type of stain before washing.
- Vinegar is a good alternative to fabric softener.
- Hairspray will remove ballpoint pen from clothing.
- To clean an iron, pour salt on a dish towel and then iron over the salt. It will clean all debris off.
- Crayon stains in clothes can be removed by soaking the article of clothing in a mixture of one box baking soda, one-half cup powdered dish soap, and hot water. Soak for six hours.
- Grass stains come out by rubbing Crisco on the spots before throwing in the washer.
- For lipstick stains, scrape off as much as you can, being careful not to rub it in. Then, blot with a cleaning solvent.
- Ring around the collar is no more! Rub with cheap hair shampoo and let it sit for a few minutes to absorb the body oils.
- Perspiration stains will disappear by dabbing a new stain with ammonia, or soaking an old stain in white vinegar for ten minutes.
- Jeans will retain their color better if washed inside out.
- Use a permanent marker to cover bleach spots on clothing.
- When ironing T-shirts with a design, turn them inside out.

- To clean fabric softener gunk from your washer and keep it smelling fresh, add a cup of household vinegar to your wash once a month.
- Use hair shampoo to clean leather gloves.
- Vinegar will set a permanent crease in clothing when ironed.
- Yellowed lace can be whitened again by soaking it in sour milk.

BATHROOM

The bathroom is a place in your home that is used often. Cleaning bathrooms can be a constant chore. The bathroom should be a place of comfort. Nothing feels better than a hot shower on a cold day, or getting clean after working hard.

Bathroom Tips
- Assign each person in your family a color of towel. This will cut down on the laundry, and your towel will only be used by you.
- Use hair conditioner to shave your legs. It is less expensive than shaving cream and leaves your legs smooth.
- Remove mold in showers by using Lysol toilet bowl cleaner and a toothbrush to get in cracks. Then rub Old English Lemon Oil all over, even on the shower door.
- A can of Coca-Cola inside the toilet will remove the ring around the toilet bowl.
- Alka Seltzer tablets in the toilet will remove stains.
- Clean mirrors with a mixture of vinegar and water and then wipe dry with newspapers.
- To make bathroom fixtures shine, rub with rubbing alcohol.
- Shower curtains and bath mats can be washed with bath towels. If hard water stains are on curtains, spray with Spray and Wash before throwing into the washer.
- An empty Pringles can is a good organizer for girls hair accessories. Put ponytail holders around the outside, and barrettes and brushes on the inside.
- Squeegee the walls of your shower after each use; this will cut down on cleaning time.
- Make your own all-purpose cleaner by mixing one gallon hot water, one-fourth cup ammonia, one-fourth cup vinegar, and one tablespoon baking soda.
- To clean stains on porcelain, when wet, rub with baking soda.

- Hair shampoo is great for cleaning shower doors and walls.
- To keep shower doors shiny and clear, use a soft cloth moistened with baby oil. It prevents scum buildup and water spots.

BEDROOMS

Bedrooms should be a place of peace and tranquility for everyone in the family. Remove televisions and computers from children's bedrooms. De-clutter the bedroom often by going through clothing and removing the items your children do not wear anymore, or what they have grown out of. Keep a bulletin board in children's rooms to post artwork or upcoming events. Let children choose a theme for their room; they are more apt to keep their room clean if they choose what they want to decorate with. Make a corner of the room a place for study. Display the covers of books and stock a desk with essential school supplies. Let your children know that reading and school work is important to you.

Bedroom Tips
- To magically remove fingerprints from walls, gently pat the smudges with a wad of crustless bread. It'll instantly soak up dirt and oils left by skin.
- Purchase bags for extracurricular activities. For example, the night before soccer practice ask if the soccer bag is packed. That way, all they have to remember in the morning is the bag.
- Give yourself extra hanging space in your closet by hanging a second rod near the ceiling. Hang your most-often worn items on the lower rod; hang your rarely-worn items on the higher rod.
- Put a chest of drawers in your closet to keep folded clothes near coordinating hanging garments and to free up space in a small bedroom.
- Purchase some over-the-door hooks to instantly create extra hanging space without a hammer or nails.
- Baskets make handy bins for small items.
- Go through all your clothes and weed out everything you haven't worn in a year.
- Store out-of-season clothes away from your closet. Under the bed is a good place for garment boxes.
- Select see-through containers to help you more easily find things you have stored. Label the containers with a 3x5 index card listing what is stored inside.

- Don't stack T-shirts and sweaters so high that they will topple over.
- Purchase a shoe organizer to keep shoes organized.
- When changing sheets, vacuum the mattress and pillows. Place a fabric softener sheet under the mattress pad to keep linens smelling fresh.
- Take pictures of your child with their artwork. This is a great way to remember the artwork without taking up storage space.
- Frame special artwork. You could take photographs of your child actually doing the artwork and then frame the finished project with the photographs.
- To clean mini blinds, purchase cotton gloves. On one hand spray the glove with cleaner and wipe the blinds. Use a dry glove on the other hand to dry the blinds.
- Keep shoelaces tied by double knotting and then wetting the laces. After they dry, they won't come undone.
- Turn off the TV and get back into books. Make reading part of your child's bedtime routine.
- Create cubbies for storing books and sports gear. Get your kids in the habit of putting things in their cubby when they get home.
- Create zones in your closets and put like items together. For example, have zones for active wear, seasonal items, accessories, and shoes.
- Label everything in your closet. Use containers that are alike to make your closet more pleasing to the eye.
- Create a weekly clean-up routine to keep your closet organized and looking fresh.

FAMILY ROOM AND LIVING ROOM

A family room should be a comfortable, inviting room where your family spends a good deal of time. Look around your room and ask yourself: Does this room make me feel good? Is there something in this room that describes what I value most? Do the decorations and items in this room bring a feeling of peace and love? If the answer to any of these questions is no, then change the room so you can answer yes!

Family Room and Living Room Tips
- Go through your music and movies. Are there any that make you feel uneasy? Get rid of any that are in question.

- Keep your computer in a high-traffic area. You will be able to see what your children are looking at and monitor the time they spend on the computer.
- Display pictures of what you believe in around your living room and family room. These will help you and your family remember what you stand for.
- Set up a corner of the room where you display books, scrapbooks, picture books, scriptures, and magazines. When you sit down, you will have something of value to look at and read.
- Limit TV time and computer time, and replace that time with playing games or reading.
- Find a place to store blankets and pillows so you can lounge around in comfort.

ENTRYWAY

The entry is the first thing you, your family, and your guests see as they come into your home. Have your entry make a statement as to who you are and what you believe. Clean off your front porch, and wash the doors and windows in your entryway. It will make your whole home seem cleaner.

Entryway Tips
- Purchase a plug-in air freshener to put near your entry; when guests arrive, it will give off a fresh, inviting scent.
- Put rugs outside your door and in your entryway to cut down on dirt being tracked in.
- Sweep and vacuum your entryway inside and out once a week, to keep up with the dirt coming in.
- Display items that you love and are interested in. Remember, this is the place where most of the people who enter your home will see. Make a statement about who you are.

STORAGE ROOM AND MISCELLANEOUS

Storage rooms are very useful, but can get overcrowded and cluttered. Avoid getting too many of one thing. Keep your containers in your storage room labeled to make things easier to find.

Storage Room and Miscellaneous Tips
- Rotate cans of food by putting the new cans in the back and moving the old cans to the front.

- Use empty detergent boxes as magazine organizers and file holders.
- To keep bugs away, mix garlic, hot peppers, and water in blender. Pour the mixture into a spray bottle and apply to plants. You can also put hot sauce on a cotton ball and place it in a houseplant to repel bugs and pests.
- Mix vinegar with cloves and cinnamon for a homemade room freshener.
- To make candles last longer, freeze them.
- If the light in your flashlight gets dim, use an emery board to sand down the ends of the batteries to get some extra life.
- Leather will dry out if stored in plastic. Store leather items in old pillowcases instead.
- In addition to mothballs, put some whole cloves in your wool coat pockets and sweater bags.
- Prevent dampness in storage rooms by punching holes in cans and filling with charcoal.
- For foggy windows and windshields, buy a chalkboard eraser. When the windows fog, just rub with the eraser! This works better than a cloth does.
- Wax closet rods to make hangers slide more easily.
- Add a little vinegar in your water when watering houseplants. This helps keep the soil sweet, and lightly on the acidic side, which is preferred by most plants.
- Rub rusty metal with pure cider vinegar. Let it dry for several days and then wipe away any remaining rust particles.
- No sponge? Use an old pair of nylons to scrub the bathroom.
- To keep mice out of your attic or garage, place moth balls around the perimeter. This also seems to discourage spiders.
- A great homemade bug killer can be made by mixing one cup sugar, one cup vinegar, and a banana peel in a plastic jug, and hanging the open jug in a tree. It will attract and trap the bugs.
- To clear soot from your chimney, save potato peelings until you have a good amount. Dry the peelings and burn them in your fireplace. They carry the soot right up and out the chimney.
- Rust stains from metal outdoor furniture can be removed from concrete by rubbing with lemon juice and a soft linen cloth.

Author's Note

Making Yours a Phenomenal Family

I would like to thank you for purchasing this book. My hope is that you will find ideas that will work for you and your family. I recognize that all families are different; what works for my family may not work for yours.

These ideas, tips, and traditions have been compiled into one book that you can go to for a new idea. I hope you will have as much fun implementing them as I have.

This book can be used as a springboard to help you plan and organize family time. Whether you would like to play a new game with your family, spend one on one time with your child or spouse, or make mealtime magical.

I would like to hear how you have used these ideas in your family. If you would like to share your experiences with me, please email me at mitzbitz1@gmail.com

I hope this book will be a quick resource in putting your family first in your life.

About the Author

Mitzi Montgomery Deeter grew up in Liberty, Utah. She attended Utah State University, where she earned her degree in nursing, and where she met and married her husband, Brian.

They returned to Liberty in 1996. They have four wonderful children, Allyson, Karlee, Lynzi, and Dustin.

Mitzi has always enjoyed spending time with family, cooking, reading, and planning and throwing parties.

She coauthored two previous books, *Faith in God Activities* and *Personal Progress Activities*.

Mitzi Deeter can be contacted through her personal website at www.mitzfamilybitz.com

0 26575 51982 2